HOW ON EARTH ?

RONALD ORENSTEIN

HOW ON EARTH?

A QUESTION-AND-ANSWER BOOK
ABOUT HOW ANIMALS AND PLANTS LIVE

Voyageur Press

For Randy and Jenny

Photography Credits

© Brian Beck, 91 bottom; © Fred Bruemmer, 15 top, 43 top, 49 left; © Ralph Brunner, 49 right; © John Cancalosi, 85 top; © M. Brock Fenton, 23; © J.A. Kraulis, 10, 52; © Aubrey Lang and Wayne Lynch, 58; © Wayne Lankinen, 18; © Wayne Lynch, 70 left; © Ron Orenstein, 33; © George Peck, 89 bottom; © J.D. Taylor, 50; © Jonathan Scott/Planet Earth Pictures, 88; © Tony Stone Worldwide, cover, 2.

The remaining copyrighted photographs were supplied by First Light Associated Photographers: Kelvin Aitken, 5 center, 7, 15, 17, 25 bottom, 46, 47, 51 top, 62, 63 left, 63 right; Annie Griffiths Belt, 4, 39 left; Mark Burnham, 57; J. Cancalosi, 16 right; W. Perry Conway, 80, 81 bottom; Ralph Clevenger, 29 top, 43 bottom, 67 bottom; George D. Dodge, Kathleen M. Dodge, Dale R. Thompson, 10 right, 10 bottom, 13 left, 27 left, 29 bottom, 30, 31, 38, 69 top, 69 bottom, 75 right, 76, 83; Bill Dow, 77 top; M. and C. Ederegger, 51 bottom; Warren and Genny Garst, 45; Dawn Goss, 12; Richard Hartmier, 89 top; Carl Haycock, 48 right; D. and J. Heaton, 79 top, 84, 85 bottom; W. H. Hodge, 19; Stephen Homer, 14, 26, 28, 67 top; Steve Kaufman, 5 left, 8, 9; Thomas Kitchin, 10, 27 right, 39, 53 top, 53 bottom, 55, 64, 65 top, 71, 90; Herbert Lange, 74 left; Robert Lankinen, 20, 37; Alan Marsh, 78; Brian Milne, 5 right, 22, 34, 36, 59 top, 59 bottom, 65 bottom, 86, 87; Peter McLeod, 41; Patrick Morrow, 44; Hans Pfletschinger, 35 bottom; Charles Philip, 82; Phototake, 16 left; Dave Reede, 92; Ed Reschke, 6, 24, 25 top; Bill Ross, 1, 32; Jeffrey L. Rotman, 27 bottom; Leonard Lee Rue III, 79 bottom; Ron Sanford, 75 top; Kevin Schafer, 77 bottom; Ron Watts, 21, 42, 56, 81 top; Wayne Wegner, 70 bottom; Martin Wendler, 66; Darwin Wiggett, 91 top; Doug Wilson, 13 right; Norbert Wu, 48 left; Gunter Ziesler, 35 top.

Design: Scott Richardson
Illustrations: Angela Vaculik

Copyright © 1994 by Ronald Orenstein

Printed and bound in Hong Kong

94 95 96 97 98 5 4 3 2 1

First published in Canada by
Key Porter Books
70 The Esplanade
Toronto, ONT M5E 1R2

Library of Congress
Cataloging-in-Publication Data

Orenstein, Ronald I. (Ronald Isaac), 1946–
How on earth?: a question-and-answer book
about how animals and plants
live / Ronald Orenstein.
p. cm.
Includes bibliographical references and index.
ISBN 0-89658-257-4
1. Natural history—Miscellanea—Juvenile
literature. 2. Biotic communities—Miscellanea—Juvenile literature. [1. Natural history—
Miscellanea. 2. Questions and answers.]
I. Title.
QH48.074 1994   94-13927
574—dc20   CIP
                                              AC

Published in the United States by
Voyageur Press, Inc.
P.O. Box 338, 123 North Second Street,
Stillwater, MN 55082 U.S.A.
612-430-2210, fax 612-430-2211

Contents

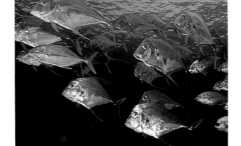

ANIMALS AND PLANTS

COMMUNITIES

MAKING ROOM FOR WILDLIFE

Acknowledgments

No one is an expert on everything. While I was writing this book, I was lucky enough to get help from experts on many kinds of animals and plants, and on the ways to help them survive. I would like to thank them. They are: M. Brock Fenton, Eugenie Clark, Don Davis, Michael Day, Anne Doncaster, Gail Foreman, Roger Fouts, R. Allan Gardner, Valerius Geist, Christine Janis, Barry Kent MacKay, Katherine Scott, Lindy Stacker, Ronald Tilson, Warren Wagner, Chris Wiggins, and the Department of Invertebrate Zoology, Royal Ontario Museum. Parts of this book were read over by Faith Campbell, Robert Johnson, Dael Morris, Jeheskel Shoshani, and Richard Winterbottom. If I've made any mistakes, though, they are my fault (and that includes leaving anyone out of this list!)

Thanks, too, to Scott Richardson and, especially, my editor Laurie Coulter at Key Porter Books, and to the staff at First Light who helped me select the photographs.

My family and friends helped, too. A special thank you to my dear friend Kaaren Dickson and her daughter Kathleen Dickson Overs, who loves frogs. As for my parents Charles and Mary Orenstein, my sister Eve Dexter, and especially my children Randy and Jenny – no thanks can ever be enough. To finish this book, I needed them all.

Introduction

How on Earth? is a book of questions and answers about the way animals and plants live. Some of the questions may be ones you have asked yourself. Others may tell you about creatures you have never heard of.

Everybody studies nature in his or her own way. Some people are interested in a favorite animal or plant. Others study the way many different kinds of animals do one thing, like find food, or fly, or take care of their babies. Still others study the animals and plants from just one part of the world.

No matter where you start, your journey through nature is bound to lead you in all sorts of interesting directions. This book is designed to help you do just that. You can start at the beginning and read it all the way through. Or you can start anywhere you like, with something that you find interesting. Wherever you start, though, look for questions that are answered on other pages. You can follow these questions back and forth through the book, exploring as you go.

Unfortunately, knowing about nature isn't enough anymore. Today, thousands of kinds of animals and plants are in danger. As you read *How on Earth?*, keep your eyes open for hints about ways you can protect wildlife.

And don't stop there. No one can tell you everything there is to know about nature. Keep reading and learning. You may be interested in *How on Earth? A Question-and-Answer Book about How Our Planet Works.* It is about the earth itself, and about how life started and grew to produce the wonderful animals and plants that live on our planet.

One more thing. There are many questions about nature that we haven't been able to answer yet. I hope that some of you will be the ones to answer them!

ANIMALS
and PLANTS

Body Plans

THREE-ROWED SEA CUCUMBER (*ISOSTICHOPUS BADIONOTUS*), BERMUDA, FLORIDA AND THE CARIBBEAN

Animal bodies are made of tiny jelly-like parts called cells. They are so small that you would need a microscope to see them. Each cell has a different job to do, and it has to be in the right place to do it. For example, an eye cell won't do you much good unless it's part of your eye.

The way an animal's cells are arranged is called its body plan. Animals have different kinds of body plans. Some animals, like people, have a head at one end. Others, like a starfish, have no head at all. The wonderful thing about body plans is that each one can develop into many very different-looking, and acting, creatures.

AGGREGATE ANEMONES (*ANTHOPLEURA ELEGANTISSIMA*), PACIFIC COAST OF NORTH AMERICA

PREVIOUS PAGES:
JAPANESE CRANES (*GRUS JAPONENSIS*), JAPAN, CHINA AND SIBERIA

■ WHY ARE ANIMALS MADE OF MANY CELLS?
An animal made of many cells can grow larger than an animal with only one cell. The bigger you are, the harder it is for other animals to eat you.
We need different kinds of cells so the parts of our body can do their jobs. We have brain cells in our brain, blood cells in our blood and taste cells in our tongues. But a simple animal like this sea anemone doesn't have a brain, or blood or a tongue.

The first living things had only one cell. One reason early animals developed, or evolved, separate cells may have been to avoid being eaten. The first predators must have been tiny, so one way to escape them was to grow too big to swallow.

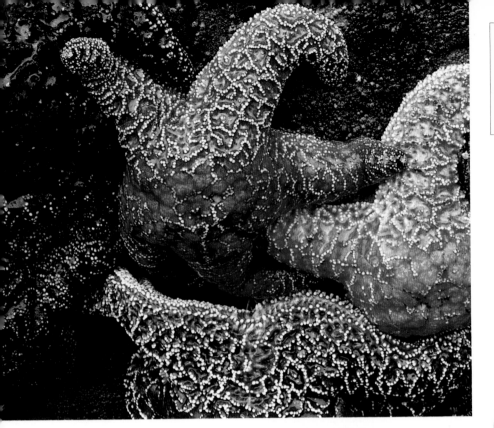

PURPLE STARFISH *(PISASTER OCHRACEUS)*, PACIFIC COAST OF NORTH AMERICA

WHAT ABOUT...?
Why does the crown-of-thorns starfish stick its stomach out of its mouth?
See page 63.

LONG-NOSED TREE SNAKE *(AHAETULLA PRASINA)*, SOUTHEAST ASIA

▲ WHY IS A STARFISH SHAPED LIKE A STAR?
The star shape of a starfish may make its body armor stronger.

Worms, snails, insects and people have right and left sides. Starfishes don't. Their bodies are arranged in a circle like the spokes of an umbrella. A starfish's skeleton is made of separate sections, or plates, linked together like an old suit of chain-mail armor. A star shape may make all the plates fit together in the strongest way.

If a fish bites off one of a starfish's five arms, the starfish can grow a new one. Its cousin the sea cucumber has an even stranger trick. If a fish attacks it, it can spit out part of its intestines. While the fish eats them, the sea cucumber crawls off to grow new ones.

▼ WHERE DOES AN INSECT WEAR ITS SKELETON?
An insect wears its skeleton on the outside of its body. It protects the insect's heart, stomach and other soft parts.

Insects and their relatives, such as lobsters and spiders, have a suit of armor instead of a skeleton inside their bodies. Because their skeleton surrounds the body, like a tube, it is much stronger than the set of bones that make up our skeleton. There is one problem with a suit of armor, though. Its owner must shed it, and grow a new one, to get any bigger.

The insect body plan has helped insects become very successful. There are more kinds of insects than of all other animals put together.

▲ WHAT ARE VERTEBRATES?
Vertebrates have skeletons on the inside of their bodies that protect their brains and spinal cords. We are vertebrates.

Vertebrates all have a hollow spinal cord running down their backs. It is usually protected by a backbone made of separate pieces of bone called vertebrae. However, sharks and some other fishes have skeletons of cartilage — like the material in your earlobe — instead of bone. The only parts of a vertebrate skeleton that can be seen are things like antlers, teeth and turtle shells.

The vertebrate body plan has evolved into more shapes and sizes than any other. Fishes, frogs, snakes, birds, mice, elephants and people all share it.

BROAD-WINGED KATYDID *(MICROCENTRUM RHOMBIFOLIUM)*, NORTH AMERICA

Plants Have Bodies, Too

Plant bodies are made up of cells, just like animal bodies. But plant cells are very different from animal cells. For example, they have a solid outer wall made of cellulose, the material that makes celery hard to chew. Animal cells have no cellulose at all.

Your body is made up of organs, such as your skin, your heart and your stomach. The leaves, roots and stems of plants are organs, too. Like animal organs, each is made of cells, and each has a job to do for the plant.

BLACK CABBAGE-TREE *(MELANODENDRON INTEGRIFOLIUM)*, ST. HELENA ISLAND

◄ **WHAT ARE PLANT BODIES LIKE?**
Plants usually have leaves, roots, flowers and stems.
This trillium is a typical plant. Its leaves make food and take in oxygen from the air. Its roots take up water and minerals and store food over the winter. Its flowers produce seeds. Its stem supports it and carries food, water and other things it needs back and forth.

In other plants, these organs do different jobs. Leaves have evolved into spines, climbing tools and insect traps. Stems can make food, store water or even strangle other plants. Plants are successful because they are able to evolve new forms, from tiny duckweeds to giant redwoods.

LARGE-FLOWERED TRILLIUM *(TRILLIUM GRANDIFLORUM)*, EASTERN NORTH AMERICA

WHAT ABOUT...?
What are flowers for?
See page 37.

▶ WHAT IS A MUSHROOM?
A mushroom is the part of a fungus that grows above the ground. The rest of the fungus is an underground mass of threads.

A mushroom is a fruiting body — the part of a fungus that carries its powdery spores. When the spores are ripe, they blow away and grow into new fungi. The rest of the fungus is a mass of slender branching threads called a mycelium.

The mycelium of some fungi can grow to giant size. One fungus in Washington State, USA, may cover 600 ha (1500 acres).

Fungi are not plants. They are members of a separate kingdom, like animals. Unlike plants, they can't make their own food or store it as starch. Instead, their mycelia take in food from the rotting bodies of dead plants or animals.

▶ WHY ARE THERE TREES?
Trees can lift their leaves above other plants to reach more sunlight.

Plants compete for sunlight. Other plants can't shade a plant's leaves if it is the tallest plant around. The taller it is, the farther the wind can blow its pollen or seeds. Birds and other animals are also more likely to visit its flowers or fruit if it is easy to see.

Trees have evolved over and over again. Many kinds of plants reach tree size. On some faraway islands, there are no ordinary trees. There, cousins of normally small plants have become trees. The cabbage-trees of St. Helena Island in the South Atlantic, for example, evolved from cousins of the daisies.

REDWOOD *(SEQUOIA SEMPERVIRENS)*, COASTAL CALIFORNIA, USA

Fitting In

NORTHERN ELEPHANT SEAL *(MIROUNGA ANGUSTIROSTRIS)*, COASTAL CALIFORNIA, USA

Our world is always changing. Living things change, too, generation after generation. Over thousands or millions of years, forests may become deserts, warm waters may cool, or islands may rise from the sea. Adaptation is the way animals and plants change to fit in with the changing world. Only the changes that make them fit in better will survive.

Millions of years ago, the ancestors of these three creatures were land animals. They have become adapted to finding their food in the sea. The dolphin has changed so much that it cannot return to the land at all.

▶ **WHY DID THIS PUFFIN CATCH SO MANY FISH AT ONE TIME? Puffins feed fish to their babies. They hunt at sea, but nest on land. Catching several fish at a time saves trips back and forth from the sea.**
How did this puffin hold on to one fish while it caught the next? The answer is an adaptation: it can hold the first fish against the rough edge of its bill with its tongue while it catches the second. A puffin can catch up to thirty small fish at a time.

Puffins can fly. Once they had a much bigger relative, the great auk, that couldn't fly. This made it easy for people to hunt great auks. The last one was killed in 1844.

ATLANTIC PUFFIN *(FRATERCULA ARCTICA)*, NORTH ATLANTIC OCEAN

WHAT ABOUT...?
What do whales and penguins eat?
See pages 48-49.

HARP SEAL MOTHER AND PUP *(PHOCA GROENLANDICA)*,
NORTH ATLANTIC OCEAN

▲ HOW CAN SEALS STAY UNDERWATER FOR SO LONG?
Seals can store oxygen in their muscles and blood to use on long, deep dives.

Seals are deep divers. Elephant seals can dive to 1600 m (5000 feet) and stay under for two hours. How do they do it?

Not by holding their breath – seals breathe out before they dive. Instead, their blood and muscles are adapted to hold large amounts of oxygen. To save oxygen, they slow down their hearts from around one hundred beats per minute to as few as four. They also close off blood vessels, so blood only goes to the brain and heart, which need fresh oxygen much more than the swimming muscles.

Seals don't have to think about not breathing underwater. They can even sleep there. When they are asleep, they come to the surface every twenty minutes or so for a breath without waking up.

▼ HOW DO DOLPHINS FIND THEIR WAY AROUND UNDER- WATER?
Dolphins can see well underwater, but they usually use echoes to tell where they are going.

Sound travels better than light underwater. This is why dolphins use their ears more often than their eyes to find their way around.

Dolphins make high-pitched clicks, probably using a fatty bulge in their forehead, the melon, to make the sound travel where they want it to go. They listen to the echoes as the sound waves bounce off rocks, fish, ice floes or other objects. They can catch food, keep from bumping into things and find their way around better this way than if they used sight alone.

ATLANTIC SPOTTED DOLPHIN *(STENELLA FRONTALIS)*, WARM WATERS OF THE ATLANTIC OCEAN

Strange Senses

Our senses – sight, hearing, taste, smell and touch – tell us about the world. For many animals, though, the world must seem very different from the way it does to us. Bees see colors that we can't see. Elephants call to one another with sounds so low we can't hear them. Fishes can sense vibrations in the water. Moths can pick up the faintest of smells with their antennae.

Senses give animals the information they need to find food, hide from enemies or get along with their own kind. Each animal's senses are adaptations to its own way of life.

WESTERN PYGMY-POSSUM *(CERCARTETUS CONCINNUS)*, SOUTHWESTERN AUSTRALIA

▼ WHAT DO INSECTS SEE?

Insects may see the world as a set of colored dots. Together, the dots make up a picture.

Did you ever wonder why it is so hard to catch a fly? One reason is that insect eyes are very good at seeing even the smallest movement.

Unlike our eyes, their huge compound eyes are made up of thousands of tiny lenses called facets. Each facet can only see a small area in front of it. What insects see may look more like a set of dots. If anything moves close to the insect, some of the dots change color. When that happens, the insect senses that it may be in danger and gets out of the way fast. Scientists now think insect brains may even be able to turn the dots into a picture something like the one we see.

HORSEFLY (FAMILY TABANIDAE)

▲ HOW DO NOCTURNAL MAMMALS SENSE THE WORLD AT NIGHT?

Large eyes, sharp ears, a good nose and long whiskers help small mammals in the dark.

This western pygmy-possum is the size of a mouse. It is nocturnal – it sleeps during the day, and looks for food at night.

Like many small night animals, it has large eyes to take in as much light as possible. Its sharp ears can turn back and forth to pick up faint sounds that may warn it of enemies. A good sense of smell helps it find flowers, where it eats pollen and nectar, and its long, sensitive whiskers help it feel its way about. The pygmy-possum must use all its senses to survive.

WHAT ABOUT...?
What do whale sharks eat?
See page 25.

GREAT WHITE SHARK *(CARCHARODON CARCHARIAS)*, WORLDWIDE

▲ HOW DO SHARKS FIND THEIR PREY?

One way that sharks find their prey is by smell. If an animal is hurt, they can find it by smelling just a few drops of its blood in the water.

Besides having a sharp sense of smell, a shark has good eyes and two sense organs we don't have at all. It has a lateral line, running along its side and over its head, to pick up the vibrations of its prey moving through the water. It also has jelly-filled canals in its head that can pick up very weak electric currents. Since muscles make tiny electric currents when they work, a shark can find an animal even if it is hidden under the sand.

■ WHAT ANIMALS TASTE WITH THEIR FEET?

Flies, butterflies and other insects taste with the bottoms of their feet. That way, they know if what they are standing on is worth eating.

Insects are so small that their food is often much bigger than they are. If a fly lands on a piece of meat, or if a butterfly lands on a flower, it needs to know if it is in the right spot for lunch. Being able to taste with its feet gives it the information it needs right away.

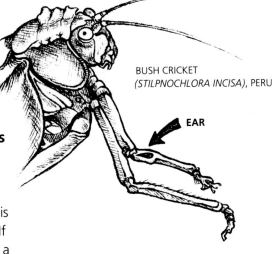

BUSH CRICKET
(STILPNOCHLORA INCISA), PERU

EAR

Crickets have another sense organ in an odd place. Their ears are on their front legs. That seems odd to us, but it seems to work fine for crickets!

A New Leaf

Adaptation doesn't just happen to animals. It can change a part of a plant's body into something very different, too. Did you know, for example, that cactus spines are leaves? So are the traps of a Venus flytrap, the bright red "petals" of a poinsettia and the needles of a spruce tree.

Leaves usually help plants get rid of extra water, but in the desert plants need to keep all the water they can find. The leaves of the desert plants in these photographs have changed, over millions of years, to help them do just that.

NORWAY SPRUCE *(PICEA ABIES)* BRANCH, EUROPE

SAGUARO CACTUS *(CARNEGIA GIGANTEA)* AND WHITE-WINGED DOVE *(ZENAIDA ASIATICA)*, SOUTHWESTERN USA AND MEXICO

◀ **WHAT ARE CACTUS SPINES? The spines of a cactus are its leaves. They protect it from enemies and help it save water.**

Many desert plants, like cacti, store water in thick, fleshy stems. But the desert sun can dry them out, and animals may try to eat the stems to get water. Cactus spines help protect the plant's water supply.

The spines are really leaves that have been changed by evolution over millions of years. Because they don't have stomates, spines don't lose water the way other leaves do. Thirsty animals may think twice before biting into their sharp points.

Some desert birds, such as the cactus wren, build their nests deep in a cactus thicket. The spines protect their babies from enemies.

STONE PLANT *(LITHOPS TURBINIFORMIS)*, SOUTHWESTERN AFRICA

▲ **WHAT ARE "LIVING STONES"?**
Stones cover the deserts of southwestern Africa, but not all of them are made of rock. African stone plants have leaves that look like pebbles.
Stone plants grow only two leaves a year. The fleshy leaves store water for the plant, and, like other leaves, they make food with sunlight.

Most of each leaf is underground, but a "window" on top of the leaf lets sunlight reach inside. The part that shows above the ground is the same color as the pebbles around it. Hungry animals have to look hard to find stone plants to eat.

■ **WHAT ARE LEAVES USUALLY FOR?**
Leaves take in oxygen from the air, make food for the plant and help it keep or get rid of water.
The green color in leaves comes from chlorophyll. Chlorophyll takes up energy from sunlight. The plant uses the energy to make food from water and carbon dioxide.

Oxygen and carbon dioxide move in and out of each leaf through tiny pits called stomates. Stomates are so small that you would need a microscope to see them. Water vapor also moves out of the stomates. As water moves out of the leaves, fresh water is pulled into the plant through its roots.

Stomates are usually on the bottom of a leaf, shaded from the sun. If they were on top, they might lose water too quickly on a hot day. That could make the plant wilt.

WHAT ABOUT...?
How do autumn leaves change color?
See page 53.

Horns and Antlers

Many animals, from beetles to dinosaurs, have horns. But the horns of antelopes, sheep and cattle have a center made of bone. The bone is covered with a layer of keratin. This is the same material that makes up your fingernails.

Only deer have antlers. Antlers are made of solid bone. Though the horns of most animals last a lifetime, deer shed their old antlers and grow a new set every year. New antlers are covered with fuzzy skin, called velvet. Once the antlers are fully grown, the velvet falls off. The antlers may be red at first, but soon turn brown.

REINDEER OR CARIBOU *(RANGIFER TARANDUS)*, NORTHERN NORTH AMERICA, EUROPE AND ASIA

RED DEER *(CERVUS ELAPHUS)*, EUROPE AND ASIA

▲ WHY DO DEER SHED THEIR ANTLERS?
Antlers have no hard covering to protect them. They wear out faster than horns and need to be replaced each year.
It's not easy to grow antlers. Deer must eat a lot of extra food to grow so much bone. They may even chew on old fallen antlers to get the calcium they need. (Calcium is the same mineral you get by drinking milk.) Why then do deer bother growing new antlers every year?

When new antlers stop growing, the bone cells they are made of start to die. Because antlers are not covered with a layer of horn to protect them from the weather, the dead bone slowly crumbles. Besides wearing out, antlers may be broken in fights. Broken antlers don't heal. Growing a new set solves the problem.

▲ WHY DO ANIMALS HAVE HORNS OR ANTLERS?
Males use their horns or antlers to fight each other.
The winners of a fight can chase the losers away from the best feeding spots. That way, the winners may get more to eat than the losers. More food means they are able to grow bigger horns.

In the breeding season, a female may look for a male with large horns or antlers. She needs to mate with a well-fed, healthy male, so her babies will be strong enough to run from their enemies as soon as they are born.

Why do female antelope, sheep and cattle need horns? They may need them to fight males for space on the feeding grounds.

WHAT ABOUT...?
What animal had a fossil cousin with six horns?
See page 75.

HARTEBEEST
(ALCELAPHUS BUSELAPHUS),
AFRICA SOUTH OF THE SAHARA

SABLE
(HIPPOTRAGUS NIGER),
EASTERN AND
SOUTHERN AFRICA

IMPALA *(AEPYCEROS MELAMPUS),* EASTERN AND SOUTHERN AFRICA

VAAL RHEBOK
(PELEA CAPREOLUS),
SOUTH AFRICA

BLACK WILDEBEEST
(CONNOCHAETES GNOU),
SOUTH AFRICA

GREATER KUDU
(TRAGELAPHUS STREPSICEROS),
EASTERN AND SOUTHERN AFRICA

ORYX
(ORYX GAZELLA), EASTERN AND SOUTHWESTERN AFRICA

■ WHY DO BIG ANTELOPES HAVE SUCH FANCY HORNS?
Horns with fancy shapes let males fight without hurting each other.

Antelopes rarely get injured in a fight. But did you know that little antelopes are more likely to hurt each other than big ones? That is because small antelopes, such as the oribi and rhebok, have short, straight horns, like spikes. They can be dangerous stabbing weapons.

Larger antelopes often have spectacular horns. Instead of stabbing with them, males lock horns and wrestle or shove each other. Each species has its own way of wrestling. The fancy shapes of their horns help them lock together more easily. Sometimes this works too well. Gazelles may get their horns locked together so tightly that they can't get loose, and both of the fighters starve to death.

How to Fly

People have dreamed of flying for centuries, but some animals have been doing it for millions of years. Flight has evolved four times. First came the insects, which took to the air about 300 million years ago. Next, the pterosaurs, or flying reptiles, took flight 220 million years ago, only to vanish with the dinosaurs. Birds appeared 140 million years ago, and, finally, the bats flew into the night skies between 70 and 100 million years ago.

SNOW GOOSE *(ANSER CAERULESCENS),* NORTH AMERICA AND EASTERN ASIA

▼ **WHY ARE BUTTERFLY WINGS SO COLORFUL?**
Butterfly wings are covered with tiny colored scales. Their colors may help butterflies hide, or even keep enemies away. Bright colors may also help butterflies tell each other apart.
Some butterflies have patterns on their wings that look like bark or leaves. They help the butterfly hide from its enemies. Others are bad-tasting, and their bright colors warn enemies to keep away. Some butterflies are not bad-tasting, but look like the butterflies that are. They may fool predators into leaving them alone.

Butterflies may also use colors to recognize others of their own kind. Male butterflies may use their colors to warn other males of the same species to keep away. When they look for a mate, colors may help them find the right kind of female.

TIGER SWALLOWTAIL *(PTEROURUS GLAUCUS),* EASTERN NORTH AMERICA

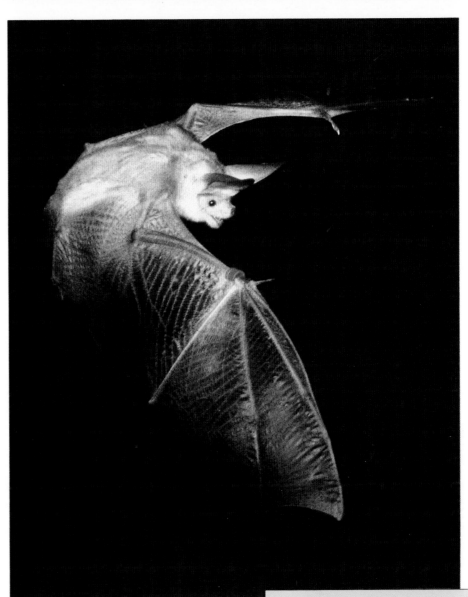

PALLID BAT *(ANTROZOUS PALLIDUS)*,
WESTERN NORTH AMERICA

▶ **WHAT DO ANIMALS NEED
TO FLY?**
**Flying animals need wings big
enough to push them through
the air, and sharp nerves and
senses to control them.**
Wings have to be big enough to
support their owner's weight in the
air. The ostrich, the largest bird in
the world, has wings that are too
small to get it off the ground. Its
fluffy wing feathers are also the
wrong shape for flying.

Support isn't enough, though.
Bats, for example, have to be able to
twist and curve their wings, so that
their flapping drives them up and
forward instead of just up. They
have to be able to steer, too –
especially bats that catch insects in
midair. Bats need sharp senses that
act like the flight instruments of an
airplane to help them fly.

WHAT ABOUT...?
Do flying frogs fly?
See page 83.

▶ **DO BATS AND BIRDS HAVE
THE SAME KIND OF WINGS?**
**Bat wings and bird wings are
very different from each other.**
If you could turn into a bird or a bat,
your arms would become your
wings. If you were a bird, your
fingers would get shorter and join
together. Long, stiff feathers,
designed for flight, would sprout on
your hands and your arms.

If you were a bat, your fingers
would grow until they were almost
as long as your arm. A web of skin
would stretch between them and
run down to your ankles and between your legs. Walking on the
ground would become hard to do.

Finding Food

Many animals eat other animals. Before they can eat them, though, they have to catch them. Hunting animals have evolved three main ways to do this. A hunter can look for its prey, and chase it down if it has to. It can sit in one spot and ambush or trap other animals that come by. Or, if it lives in the water, it can use a strainer to filter out tiny animals.

RED FOX *(VULPES VULPES)* POUNCING ON MOUSE, NORTH AMERICA, EURASIA, INTRODUCED IN AUSTRALIA

CHEETAH *(ACINONYX JUBATUS)*, CHASING HARE, AFRICA AND SOUTHWESTERN ASIA (IRAN)

WHAT ABOUT...?
How do the great whales feed?
See page 48.

▲ HOW DOES THE CHEETAH RUN SO FAST?
The cheetah is the fastest runner on earth. Its long legs and flexible spine help it run quickly.

The cheetah is adapted to run down small, fast antelopes on the grasslands of Africa and Asia.

If you are a runner, the longer your steps, the faster you can go. Cheetahs have long legs. They can also bend their spines to bring their hind legs even further forward at each bound. The pads of their toes are hard and ridged like the soles of gym shoes, and their claws grab the ground like the spikes on the bottoms of soccer boots. Their heads are small and streamlined, with wide nostrils for a good flow of air.

With this equipment, a cheetah may hit 110 km/h (68 mph) – faster than the speed limit on many highways.

CRAB SPIDER (FAMILY THOMISIDAE)

▲ WHY DO CRAB SPIDERS LIVE IN FLOWERS?
Crab spiders hide in flowers to catch visiting insects.
If you can't chase your prey, you can sit and wait for it to come to you. That is what a crab spider does. It hides in a flower, waiting for butterflies or bees to visit in search of nectar.

To make sure that it is not seen, it holds very still and changes its color to match the flower. When an insect arrives, the spider springs forward and grabs it. The spider's bite poisons its prey.

▼ HOW DOES THE WORLD'S LARGEST FISH CATCH ITS FOOD?
Whale sharks strain tiny shrimp, fish and other small animals out of the seawater.
The whale shark has thousands of small teeth, but it doesn't bite its food. Instead, it takes in enormous mouthfuls of water and drains them out through the gill openings at the back of its mouth. Its gills act like strainers, combing out everything from tiny plants to shrimp and medium-sized fish. This kind of food-gathering is called filter feeding.

Whale sharks can grow to 12 m (40 feet) in length. That's longer than a school bus. But they are not dangerous to people. In fact, divers have hitched rides on their backs!

WHALE SHARK *(RHINCODON TYPUS)* FILTER FEEDING, TROPICAL SEAS

Getting Away

Not many animals want to end up as some other animal's lunch. With so many hunters around, animals have had to evolve ways to defend themselves. Some, like the elephants, have simply become too large for most hunters to attack. Others, like deer and antelopes, use speed to escape. Still others have become experts at hiding, or, like a turtle, protect themselves by wearing armor. And some have evolved ways to fight back, with teeth, claws, spines or even stranger weapons.

SPUR-THIGHED TORTOISE *(TESTUDO GRAECA)*, SOUTHERN EUROPE, NORTH AFRICA AND THE MIDDLE EAST

SOUTHERN THREE-BANDED ARMADILLO
(TOLYPEUTES MATACUS),
SOUTHERN SOUTH AMERICA

▶ **WHY DO ARMADILLOS WEAR ARMOR?**
Armadillos wear armor to protect themselves from their enemies.
The armadillo's armor is made of bony sections, or plates, covered with horn. Their bellies, though, have no armor. Most armadillos protect their bellies by pulling in their legs and sitting tightly on the ground. Some kinds, though, can escape by quickly burying themselves.

This three-banded armadillo prefers running away to digging, but if caught, it can do a trick no other armadillo can do. It can roll itself into a ball.

WHAT ABOUT...?
Why do some caterpillars wear disguises?
See page 69.

BLISTER BEETLE (FAMILY MELOIDAE), CALIFORNIA, USA

▶ CAN A PORCUPINE "SHOOT" ITS QUILLS?

Porcupines use their quills to fight off their enemies, but they can't "shoot" them.

Porcupine quills are special, stiff hairs with sharp, barbed tips. They can't be "shot," but they come loose easily. If attacked, the porcupine fights back by swinging its tail at its enemy. The attacker may get a faceful of quills that work their way into its body. The quills can cause sores that may even kill it.

One North American predator, the fisher, has learned how to catch a porcupine. Porcupines have no quills on their undersides. The weasel-like fisher is an expert at flicking them over to get at their soft bellies.

NORTH AMERICAN PORCUPINE *(ERETHIZON DORSATUM)*, NORTH AMERICA

▲ HOW DID THE BLISTER BEETLE GET ITS NAME?

When a blister beetle is attacked, its knees start to bleed. Its blood can give you blisters if you touch it.

Many beetles defend themselves with chemical weapons. Blister beetles have a chemical in their blood that can raise blisters. When attacked, these insects start to bleed from the knees and other parts of their body. That will keep some of their enemies, like birds, away. But others, like mantises, aren't bothered by it at all.

Other beetles spray their attackers with acid. Bombardier beetles go even further. They set off explosions in their bodies that shoot puffs of hot, blistering chemicals at their enemies.

MOSES SOLE *(PARDACHIRUS MARMORATUS)*, RED SEA, INDIAN AND WEST PACIFIC OCEANS

▲ HOW DO FLATFISHES HIDE FROM THEIR ENEMIES?

Flatfishes hide by burying themselves in the sand, or changing color to match their background.

As flatfishes, such as this sole, grow, one eye moves over to the other side of their body. For the rest of their lives they swim or lie on the bottom with this side up. Soles often bury themselves in the sand, with only their eyes and gills showing.

Many flatfishes can change their color and pattern almost instantly to match any background. Some can even imitate the squares on a checkerboard! A flatfish can be almost invisible as it lies on the bottom. This Moses sole has an extra trick: the slime covering its body contains a natural shark repellent.

Poison and Venom

One way to keep from being eaten is to become impossible to eat. The bodies of poisonous animals and plants contain chemicals that make anything that eats them sick. That won't help the first one that gets eaten, but its killer will think twice before trying another. Over thousands of years, a predator may become able to eat the poison without hurting itself. The golden bamboo lemur of Madagascar, for example, eats bamboo that has enough cyanide in it to kill several people.

Venomous animals use poison to hunt. They inject it into their prey with a bite or a sting.

GOLDEN BAMBOO LEMUR *(HAPALEMUR AUREUS)*, SOUTHEASTERN MADAGASCAR

▶ **WHY ARE POISON DART FROGS SO COLORFUL?**
The bright colors of poison dart frogs warn their enemies to keep away.
The little poison dart frogs of the American tropics are easy to see on the rainforest floor. They are not just showing off. Their enemies must learn what they look like so they will not attack.

It's an important lesson for their enemies to learn. The skin of these frogs produces several deadly chemicals. One kind of poison dart frog from Colombia contains enough poison to kill ten people.

One of these poisons is also made by a bird, the hooded pitohui of New Guinea. The pitohui has the poison in its muscles as well as in its skin and feathers. Scientists don't understand why it doesn't poison itself!

STRAWBERRY POISON DART FROG
(DENDROBATES PUMILIO), CENTRAL AMERICA

WHAT ABOUT...?
Why are some rainforest plants poisonous?
See page 66.

▶ CAN ONE ANIMAL USE ANOTHER'S POISON?

Some nudibranchs eat hydroids. They can protect themselves by using the stinging cells of the hydroids in their own bodies.

Nudibranchs, or sea slugs, are ocean snails without shells. They are often very beautiful.

Some nudibranchs can make their own bad-tasting chemicals, but others steal poison from the hydroids they eat. Hydroids, which look like tiny sea anemones, have stinging cells on their tentacles that they use to kill their prey. Instead of digesting the stinging cells, the nudibranchs move them to their own backs. There are not many animals that will eat a nudibranch!

SPANISH SHAWL NUDIBRANCH *(FLABELLINOPSIS IODINEA)*, PACIFIC COAST OF NORTH AMERICA

◀ WHY DO COBRAS NEED VENOM?

Venom helps cobras catch their prey. Some cobras also spray their venom into an attacker's eyes.

Snakes don't have arms or claws to hold on to their struggling prey. Some of them, like cobras, use venom to kill quickly prey that might otherwise escape, or even hurt them.

A cobra will only bite people or other large animals in self-defense. It prefers to warn us away by spreading its hood. The African "spitting" cobras have another defense. They can spray their venom into an enemy's eyes from more than 2 m (6 feet) away.

ASIAN COBRA *(NAJA NAJA)*, TROPICAL ASIA

Insects that Eat Plants

There is hardly a plant on earth that is not eaten by an insect. Some plants are attacked by hundreds of different kinds. Every part of a plant can be an item on an insect's menu. Termites and wood borers can even eat wood.

To defend themselves, plants have evolved thorns, waxy coatings and poisons – but that doesn't stop some insects. Burnet or smoky moths use the poisons of the plants they eat to protect themselves from their own enemies.

SIX-SPOT BURNET MOTH (*ZYGAENA FILIPENDULAE*), EUROPE

> **WHAT ABOUT…?**
> **How did the blister beetle get its name?**
> See page 27.

IMMATURE LOCUSTS (ORDER ORTHOPTERA), SOUTH AMERICA

▼ **WHAT ARE LOCUSTS?**
Locusts are dry-country grass-hoppers that may swarm by the millions after it rains.
Locusts live in the warmer and drier parts of the world. Usually they stay away from one another. After heavy rains, however, there may be more plants to eat, and more locusts to eat them. As new locusts are born,

they start to change their behavior. Instead of avoiding one another, they gather in huge swarms. One swarm of African desert locusts may number 50 000 000 000 animals.

Locusts can do great harm to farmers' crops. In 1957, one swarm destroyed enough grain to feed a million people for a year.

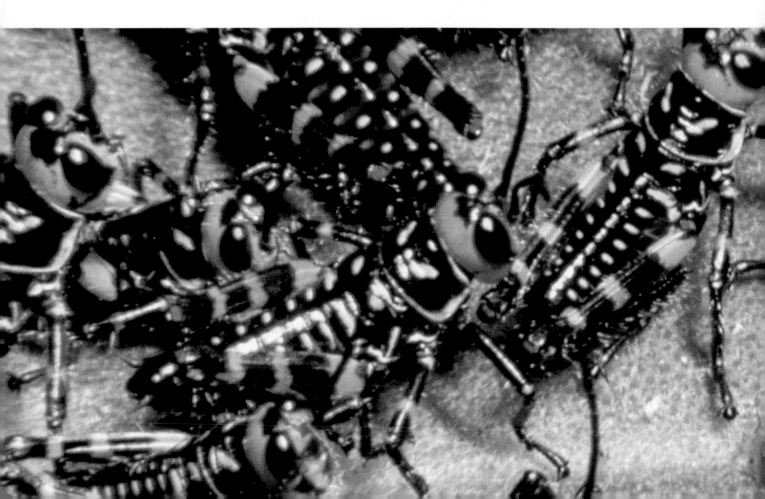

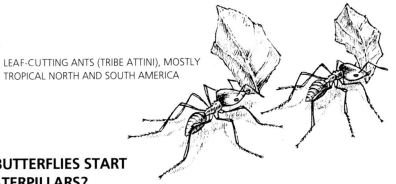

LEAF-CUTTING ANTS (TRIBE ATTINI), MOSTLY TROPICAL NORTH AND SOUTH AMERICA

■ WHY DO BUTTERFLIES START LIFE AS CATERPILLARS?
Caterpillar bodies are better for eating and growing than butterfly bodies.

Adult butterflies have to be able to find mates and good places to lay their eggs. To do this, they need wings and large eyes.

Caterpillars, however, usually hatch on the leaves they use for food. They don't have to travel far or see very well, so they don't need wings or compound eyes. Their bodies are designed for eating and growing. They only need to become adults when they are full grown and ready to mate.

Bees, flies and most other insects also have babies that look very different from their parents.

▲ WHICH INSECTS GROW THEIR OWN FOOD?
Leaf-cutting ants eat fungus that they grow themselves.

Leaf-cutting ants live in the warmer parts of North and South America. Troops of leaf-cutting ants climb into trees and cut pieces of leaf, each about the size of your thumbnail. With each ant carrying a piece of leaf, the troop marches in single file back to its underground nest.

In the nest, the ants chew the bits of leaf into tiny, soft pieces. They stick the pieces on the roof of their nest. A special fungus, which lives only in leaf-cutting ant nests, grows on the bits of leaf. The fungus is the ants' only food.

▼ HOW DO CATERPILLARS DEFEND THEMSELVES?
Some caterpillars are hard for enemies to see. Others smell bad or have stinging hairs.

Caterpillars look helpless, but they can defend themselves from the other animals that like to eat them.

Many hide by looking like twigs or bits of leaves. They can hold very still, or even sway in the breeze like a real leaf. Others, like the monarch butterfly, taste bad and wear bright colors to warn predators away. Swallowtail caterpillars can stick out a Y-shaped organ that lets off a foul smell.

Caterpillars like this one are covered with stinging hairs or spines that can inject poison into an attacker. After one bad experience, a predator will leave this kind of caterpillar alone.

CATERPILLAR (ORDER LEPIDOPTERA), SOUTH AMERICA

Plants that Eat Insects

There is no such thing as a man-eating plant, but there are plants that eat meat. Most of the 550 or so kinds of carnivorous plants in the world live in boggy areas. Because they can't get the nitrogen they need from the acid soil of bogs, they get it from insect bodies instead.

The trick is to catch the insects. To do this, plants have evolved several types of trap using their leaves. They range from the deadly jugs of the pitcher plants, to the glue-tipped hairs of the sundews, to the mousetrap leaves of the Venus flytrap.

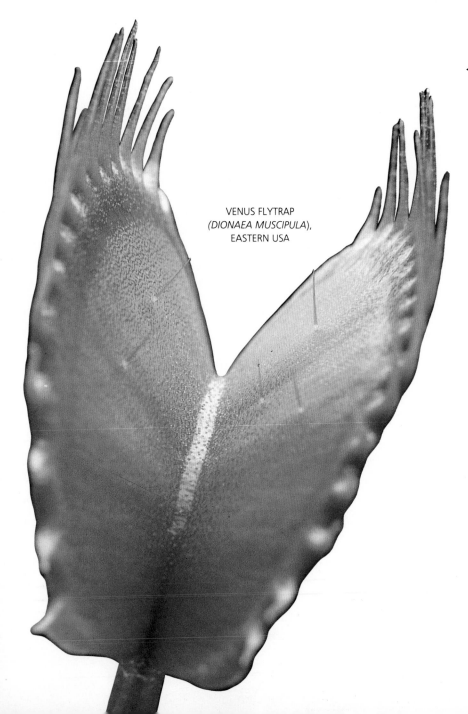

VENUS FLYTRAP
(DIONAEA MUSCIPULA),
EASTERN USA

◄ **HOW DOES THE VENUS FLYTRAP CLOSE ITS TRAP? Special cells on the outer wall of the trap can swell up with water, like balloons. This forces the trap shut.**

Plants have no nerves or muscles. How does the Venus flytrap "know" when to shut its trap, and how does it do it?

On the inner side of the trap are three trigger hairs. If an insect touches two of them, or touches one of them twice, an electrical signal travels to cells on the outer side of the trap. These cells quickly take in water and swell up. At the same time, the cells on the inside of the trap shrink. This sudden change in pressure forces the trap shut.

The long bristles around the trap act like bars on a jail cell, keeping the insect inside. The trap stays shut for several days, long enough to turn the soft parts of its prey into a nitrogen-rich liquid. The trap absorbs the liquid, then opens slowly. The hard parts of the insect fall out, and the trap is ready for another victim.

Each trap can only shut three or four times. Then it dies, and the plant grows a new one.

WHAT ABOUT...?
What are the bodies of plants like?
See page 12.

▶ HOW DO PITCHER PLANTS CATCH INSECTS?

Attracted by nectar in the plant's pitchers, insects fall into them and drown. The plant digests them.

The colorful pitchers of this plant from Borneo attract insects, which are lured inside by sweet nectar dripping from its lid. Once inside, they slip on the smooth edge of the pitcher and fall into a pool of liquid. There is no escape. Hairs on the walls of each pitcher point downward, and keep the insect from climbing out. Finally, it drowns. Chemicals flow into the pitcher and slowly digest the prey.

Pitchers make such good insect traps that three different families of plants have developed them. Southeast Asian pitchers like this one are the largest. One even contained a drowned rat!

CAN I GROW INSECT-EATING PLANTS?

With care, you can grow carnivorous plants at home, but wild ones should be left to grow where they are.

You can buy Venus flytraps, sundews, bladderworts and other carnivorous plants at many large greenhouses. Because they live in acid bogs, you should grow them in sphagnum or peat moss. Never let them dry out. A humid terrarium is a good place for them.

Unfortunately, some carnivorous plants have become rare because people have collected too many of them in the wild. If you see wild ones, leave them alone. Make sure your "pets" were grown in a nursery!

PITCHER PLANT *(NEPENTHES VILLOSA)*, MOUNT KINABALU, BORNEO

Finding a Mate

A ROOSTER DISPLAYING

Finding a mate is very important. It's the only way most animals can have babies. Some male animals, like fur seals, have to fight other males to see which one will get to mate with a female.

Many male animals have ornaments or bright colors. They may show off with fancy displays to warn off rival males or to catch a female's attention. A rooster puffing up his feathers in front of a hen is displaying.

Females may give off special smells that show when they are ready to mate. That is why male dogs will follow a female when she is in heat.

WHAT ABOUT...?
How do deep-sea anglerfish keep a mate?
See page 60.

POLYPHEMUS MOTH (*ANTHERAEA POLYPHEMUS*), EASTERN NORTH AMERICA

◄ **HOW DO MALE SILK MOTHS FIND THEIR MATES?**
Male silk moths use their feathery antennae to smell special chemicals made by the females. They can smell the females from a long way off.

Male silk moths fly about at night, looking for a female to mate with. Once they come out of their cocoon and are able to fly, that is all they do. They don't even eat.

Females have to let the males know where they are. They do this by making special chemicals called pheromones. The pheromones are released into the air, and float away on the night winds.

The huge, feathery antennae of the males are pheromone finders. If even one molecule of pheromone touches its antennae, a male can smell it. He can find the female from several kilometers (miles) away by following her trail of pheromones.

RUFFS *(PHILOMACHUS PUGNAX)*, NORTHERN EUROPE AND ASIA

▲ WHY DO RUFFS HAVE RUFFS?
The ruff is a shorebird from Eurasia. Males grow a ruff of feathers in the spring. They use it to show off to other males. The males that show off the best get to mate with the females.

In spring, male ruffs gather on a dancing ground called a lek. They spend the whole day there. Males with dark ruffs fight each other for the best spots on the lek. They raise their colorful ruffs as they show off to each other.

Females visit the lek to find a mate. They usually pick the males that have the best dancing spots.

Some of the males have white or light tan ruffs. These birds usually don't have a dancing spot. Instead, they wait for a chance to mate with a female while the other males are busy showing off.

▼ ARE EARTHWORMS MALE OR FEMALE?
Each earthworm is both male and female.

Every earthworm can lay eggs and make the sperm it needs to fertilize the eggs. But earthworms still look for mates. When two earthworms mate, they exchange sperm and store it in little pouches.

After mating, each earthworm makes a slimy tube around itself. The tube slips off the worm like a sleeve, collecting eggs and sperm as it goes. The sperm fertilizes the eggs. Once it is off the worm, the tube closes up at both ends, making a little packet in the soil for the fertilized eggs.

MATING EARTHWORMS (ORDER LUMBRICIDA)

Finding a Pollinator

Plants can't attract a mate the way animals do. Instead, many flowering plants have evolved ways to attract animal pollinators. Pollinators carry powdery yellow pollen from the male part of one flower to the female part of another flower. If the female part doesn't receive any pollen, it can't form seeds. Birds, butterflies, bees, bats and beetles are important pollinators.

You don't have to fly to be a pollinator. In southwestern Australia, a tiny marsupial, the honey possum, spends its life going from flower to flower looking for sweet nectar. Nectar is the reward plants make to attract their pollinators. Some flowers don't make nectar. Instead, they trick their pollinators into visiting them.

HONEY POSSUM OR NOOLBENGER *(TARSIPES ROSTRATUS)*, SOUTHWESTERN AUSTRALIA

▶ **HOW ARE WILLOWS POLLINATED?**
Pussy willows, grasses and many trees are pollinated by the wind.

The flowers of willows, grasses, oaks and poplars are small and not at all colorful because they don't need to attract an animal to pollinate them. They use the wind to carry their pollen away. That is why pussy willows flower early in spring, before their leaves grow big enough to block the wind.

Wind pollination works well as long as there are lots of other plants of the same species nearby. It's ideal for grasslands or temperate forests where there are only a few kinds of trees. In tropical forests, where there may be hundreds of kinds, animals are more likely to carry pollen to the right place.

PUSSY WILLOW *(SALIX DISCOLOR)*,
EASTERN NORTH AMERICA

■ HOW DO FLOWERS FOOL THEIR POLLINATORS?

Some flowers smell sweet, but have no nectar. Some are disguised as things insects want. Others set traps for insects.

Some flowers attract pollinators with false advertising. They are colorful or fragrant, but make no nectar. Others smell like rotting meat, and attract flies or beetles hunting for a meal. Some orchids even look like female wasps. They are pollinated when the male wasps try to mate with them!

Other flowers, like the Dutchman's-pipe of Europe, set traps. Its pollen may not be ready when an insect visits. Tiny gnats that land on a Dutchman's-pipe flower slip on its waxy surface and fall down a tube into a hidden chamber in the flower. Once inside, they can't climb out again because the tube is lined with downward-pointing hairs. The flower keeps them prisoner until its pollen is ready. Then it tips over, the hairs wilt and the pollen-covered gnats escape.

Some kinds of water lily flowers drown visiting insects. On the first day the flower opens, insects looking for pollen find none. But as they look, they slip on the waxy male stamens and fall into a pool of liquid at the center of the flower. The insects drown as the liquid washes off any pollen they may have picked up from older flowers. The next day, the pool is gone.

▼ HOW DO FLOWERS ATTRACT HUMMINGBIRDS?

Flowers attract tiny humming-birds with their bright colors. Hummingbirds seem to like red flowers best.

Hummingbirds have good color vision but very little sense of smell. This is why they are attracted to brightly colored flowers.

Hummingbird flowers make sweet nectar, usually deep in the flower. When the hummingbird pokes its bill into the flower to find nectar, the long male stamens brush pollen onto the feathers on its head. If it visits the same kind of flower again, the pollen is picked up by the sticky tip of the female carpel.

Some flowers are shaped like long tubes. Hummingbirds with very long bills can reach into them for nectar, but other birds can't reach the nectar, and stay away. After a hummingbird visits them, it will probably carry their pollen to the same kind of flower later on. That is just what the plant needs the bird to do.

RUFOUS HUMMINGBIRD (SELASPHORUS RUFUS), WESTERN NORTH AMERICA

WHAT ABOUT...?
What is the world's largest flower, and why does it smell so bad?
See page 83.

Animal Parents

For almost all animals, the most dangerous time of life is just after birth. If a young animal survives its first days or months, its chances of growing up and having babies of its own are much better.

Animals have two main ways of solving this problem. The first is to have so many babies that some are sure to survive. Some fishes, like cod, lay eggs by the million. The second way is to have fewer babies, but to protect them until they are able to take care of themselves. That's what scorpions, octopuses, crocodiles, birds and many other animals do. People do it, too!

▼ DO MOTHER SPIDERS MAKE GOOD PARENTS?

Most spiders lay their eggs in silken sacs. Some mother spiders guard the sac until the eggs hatch. Others take care of their babies, too.

Many mother spiders guard their eggs carefully, but ignore their young after they hatch. The mother green lynx spider, for example, spins a sac to hold her eggs, attaches it to a plant with silken threads, and then sits on guard on top of it. Other kinds of spiders carry their egg sacs around with them.

Some spiders also take care of their babies. Wolf spiders carry their babies on their backs for about a week after they hatch. A few kinds of spiders feed their young. They bring their babies dead insects or give them food they have already digested. *Coelotes* spiders go even further: in the fall, after the mother spider dies, her young eat her body.

WOLF SPIDER (*LYCOSA PALABUNDA*) WITH YOUNG, EASTERN AUSTRALIA, SOUTH SEA ISLANDS

GREEN LYNX SPIDER (*PEUCETIA VIRIDANS*) WITH EGG SAC, SOUTHERN USA, MEXICO AND CENTRAL AMERICA

▼ WHY DO MONKEYS TAKE SO LONG TO GROW UP?
Monkeys, apes and people need a long time to learn how to be adults.

As soon as they are born, some animals know everything they need to know to live on their own. Baby spiders can feed themselves, hide or spin webs. They have nothing to learn from their parents.

However, primates like this baby snow monkey – or like ourselves – have to learn how to take care of themselves, and how to get along with their families and neighbors. Young monkeys need to stay with their families for a long time so they can learn all they need to know. Their parents, and sometimes their older brothers and sisters, are their teachers.

CANADA GOOSE *(BRANTA CANADENSIS)* THREATENING A STRIPED SKUNK *(MEPHITIS MEPHITIS)*, NORTH AMERICA

SNOW MONKEY OR JAPANESE MACAQUE *(MACACA FUSCATA)*, JAPAN

▲ HOW DO GROUND-NESTING BIRDS GUARD THEIR YOUNG?
If a predator is too close to a bird's nest or young, the bird may try to chase it away. Some parent birds try to get the enemy to chase them instead.

Birds that nest on the ground have many enemies. This Canada goose is trying to frighten the skunk by spreading its wings and walking towards it in a threatening way. It may make the skunk change its mind about robbing the nest.

Instead of attacking, many shorebirds pretend to be hurt when predators get close to their nests. The predators, maybe thinking they will be easy to catch, chase them rather than look for the nest. When the enemy is far enough from its nest, the bird flies away.

WHAT ABOUT...?
What bird buries its eggs?
See page 85.

HOW CAN I LEARN BIRD SONGS?

Most species of bird have their own song. Learning bird songs is a good way to recognize birds, even if you can't see them.

The best way to learn bird songs is to go on a field trip with your family or class led by a person who knows a lot about birds. Another way to learn bird songs is to listen to a tape or record of birds singing.

You can even attract birds by playing recordings of their songs, but don't do this too often because it may keep a bird from finding food or guarding its nest.

Keeping in Touch

Most animals need to communicate with each other, even if the only time they meet is to mate or fight. They must be able to make signals that others of their own kind will understand. We usually use sounds or actions to signal each other. Other animals do, too.

Animals have other ways of communicating as well. You have probably watched dogs sniffing each other when they meet. They are sending signals by smell. Deer use a special gland on their faces to smear scent onto trees and bushes. Other deer may smell this, and will know that they are on the first deer's territory. Fireflies, on the other hand, signal each other with flashing lights.

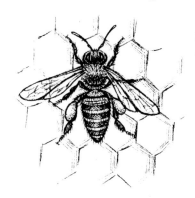

HONEYBEE (*APIS MELLIFERA*), ORIGINALLY AFRICA, EUROPE AND WESTERN ASIA

◄ HOW DO MEMBERS OF A WOLF PACK KEEP FROM FIGHTING?
Wolves in a pack sort out their differences with signals other wolves understand. That way, they don't have to fight.
Sometimes wolves fight each other to see which one will be the leader of the pack, or which one will get to mate. But wolves have sharp teeth and strong muscles. In a fight they can seriously hurt each other. This is why a pack of wolves has to be able to get along without fighting if they can.

Each wolf in a pack has its place. If one wolf challenges another, the second wolf may lay back its ears or roll over as a way of saying, "I give up." That way, they don't have to fight for position.

Wolves make many kinds of faces, sounds and actions that can tell other wolves how they are feeling. Wolf packs have one signal they all use together. This is howling. Howling may help keep the pack together, or warn other packs to stay away.

▲ WHY DO BEES DANCE?
Bees dance to show other bees in their hive where to find food.
Bees in a hive work together to gather food. If a worker bee finds some flowers, she flies back to the hive. She uses a dance to tell the other bees where the food is.

In the dance, she runs in a figure eight. When she finishes, she runs back through it in a straight line. As she heads up the middle of the eight, she waggles her body. The direction she runs shows the direction of the food, and the number of waggles show how far away it is. As she dances, the other bees crowd around and smell her body to find out what kind of flower she has been visiting.

■ WHY DO BIRDS SING?
Male birds usually sing to attract mates and to tell other males to stay away.
A bird's song carries two different messages. To female birds, it may say that a male is ready to mate. To other males, the song may mean "keep out of my territory!" Many songbirds set up areas called territories that they defend against other males. If another bird sings in its territory, a male will try to drive it away.

Some male and female birds sing duets. They may sing at the same time, or else take turns answering each other. Singing duets may help the pair stay together.

WHAT ABOUT...?
How did the skylark get its name?
See page 54.

GRAY WOLF (*CANIS LUPUS*),
NORTH AMERICA, EUROPE AND ASIA

Animal Societies

Many animals live most of their lives alone. You won't find a herd of rhinoceroses, for example. Some animals, though, live with others of their kind. Sometimes, like people, they live together in huge numbers. In these animal societies, animals spend much of their time with one another.

In some societies, animals may help each other find food or guard their babies. In others, each animal has a special job to do. They may even live their lives joined together, as coral polyps do.

TERMITE MOUND, AUSTRALIA

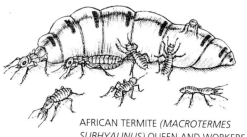

AFRICAN TERMITE *(MACROTERMES SUBHYALINUS)* QUEEN AND WORKERS, AFRICA

▶ **WHAT IS A TERMITE SOCIETY LIKE?**
A termite colony has a king, a queen and their children. The children are workers or soldiers.

Termites are social insects, like bees and ants. Each termite colony contains a king and his mate, a huge queen who may live for years. She does nothing but lay eggs. All the other termites in the colony are their children. They include workers, which build the nest, gather food and care for the babies, and soldiers, which guard the colony.

In dry tropical areas, termite colonies build huge mounds of dried earth up to 7.5 m (23 feet) high – almost as high as a two-story house. The mound is mostly hollow and helps keep the nest cool.

WHAT ABOUT...?
How do hornets build
their nests?
See page 44.

▶ WHAT ARE THESE WALRUSES DOING?
Walruses lie together in large herds. They may be keeping each other warm.

Walruses often haul out by the hundreds on a favorite beach. Even if there is plenty of room, they crowd together, resting their tusks on one another's backs. They are not particularly friendly, though. They sometimes fight for the best places.

Walruses live in the Arctic. For much of the year, lying in groups may help them keep warm. However, even in summer, when walruses have more trouble keeping cool than warming up, they still like to lie around on top of each other. Nobody knows why.

WALRUSES *(ODOBENUS ROSMARUS)*,
ARCTIC SEAS

RED SEA FAN *(MELITHAEA* SP.),
SEA OF CORTEZ, MEXICO

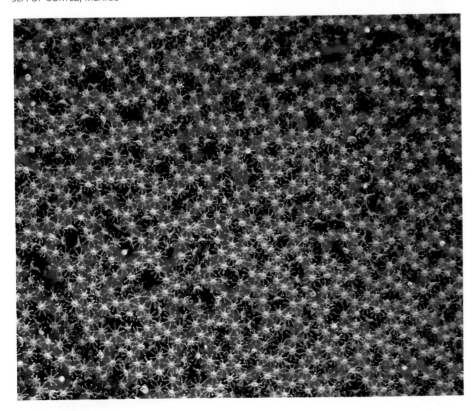

◀ WHAT ARE CORAL POLYPS?
Coral polyps are tiny animals. The polyps in a piece of coral are joined together.

Coral is made of the skeletons of tiny animals called polyps. Each polyp makes its coral skeleton as it grows, using minerals it takes from the seawater around it.

Some polyps live alone. Most kinds, though, like this sea fan, live together in colonies of thousands of animals. New polyps grow like buds from the old ones. All of them are joined together. When one feeds, the whole colony can use its food. You could even think of the colony as a single animal with thousands of mouths.

Are People Different?

We are animals, too. But are we different from other animals? For a long time people tried to find ways to prove that we were. The more we looked, though, the more we found that other animals can do many things that we thought made people special.

Some animals can use tools, build houses and even paint pictures. Of course they can't do them as well as we can, but why should that matter? Although we can do things with our brains that no other animal can do, an elephant can do things with its nose that no other animal can do!

EGYPTIAN VULTURE *(NEOPHRON PERCNOPTERUS)* SMASHING OSTRICH EGGS, AFRICA AND SOUTHERN EUROPE

▶ **CAN ANIMALS MAKE PAPER? Paper wasps chew wood pulp into paper. They use it to build their nests.**

Wasps and hornets have been making paper for millions of years. In spring, a hornet queen gathers bits of wood and plant fibers. She chews them into a pulp and uses them to build a "queen nest" for her first few eggs.

The eggs hatch into workers that add more paper to the nest. The queen stays in the nest, laying more eggs. All summer, workers make more paper and the nest grows. New queens and males are born at the end of summer, but only the queens live until the next spring.

HORNET NEST *(VESPULA* SP.), NORTH AMERICA AND EURASIA

CHIMPANZEE *(PAN TROGLODYTES)*, AFRICA SOUTH OF THE SAHARA

■ CAN ANIMALS DRAW PICTURES?
Some animals in zoos enjoy painting. They seem to understand what they are doing.

Ruby is an elephant in the Phoenix Zoo in Arizona. She likes to paint. She holds the brush in her trunk and is very careful to keep her marks on the paper. The zoo sells her paintings to raise money to save endangered species.

Some chimpanzees enjoy painting, too. A chimpanzee named Moja had learned human sign language, and when someone asked her what one of her pictures was, she made the hand sign for "bird."

▲ CAN ANIMALS USE TOOLS?
Many kinds of animals, from birds to chimpanzees, use tools. Some even make their own.

We aren't the only tool-using animals. Egyptian vultures are birds that eat dead animals or other birds' eggs. They hold stones in their beaks and use them to smash hard-shelled ostrich eggs. Other birds use twigs to pry insects loose from cracks in tree bark.

Horses have been seen using sticks as back scratchers, and chimpanzees use them as weapons.

Chimpanzees also chew clumps of leaves to make a sponge. They use the sponge to get drinking water from a stream, or a puddle on the branch of a tree.

This chimpanzee is using a grass stem or twig to probe for termites to eat. If they can't find the right kind of tool, chimpanzees will make one by stripping bark and branches from a twig until it is the right shape.

WHAT ABOUT...?
Do animals keep farms?
See page 51.

COMMUNITIES

What Is a Community?

Everywhere they live, animals and plants affect one another's lives. They may hunt each other, fight for food or a place to live, or become partners. They make up a community.

The simple, but very important, community on these two pages lives in the waters around Antarctica. Like all communities, it depends on plants that make food from sunlight and oxygen. In this case, the plants are microscopic algae that float in the surface layers of the sea. They are eaten by little animals called krill, and the krill in turn are eaten by other animals, including the largest creatures on earth.

ANTARCTIC KRILL *(EUPHAUSIA SUPERBA)*, SOUTHERN OCEANS

▲ WHAT ARE KRILL, AND WHY ARE THEY SO IMPORTANT?

Krill are tiny shrimp-like animals that live in Antarctic seas. They are food for almost all of the larger animals that live there.

Krill make up in numbers what they lack in size. Swarms of more than two million tonnes (tons) of krill have been seen in Antarctic waters.

Today, fishermen from some countries are fishing for krill. Scientists are worried about what would happen if the fishermen catch too many. Most of the larger animals in the Antarctic eat krill, including whales, seals, fishes, squid and penguins. If anything happened to the krill, the whole Antarctic community would be in trouble.

▼ WHAT DO THE GREAT WHALES EAT?

Baleen whales, such as these humpback whales, feed on krill, tiny shrimp and fish.

Humpback whales sometimes work together to surround schools of fish. They even blow "bubble nets" around the fish to keep them together. Then they lunge through the school from below, engulfing tonnes (tons) of water and fish.

Most of the great whales have no teeth. Instead, they have plates of whalebone or baleen – material something like your fingernails – in their upper jaws. The baleen acts like a strainer, draining the water away while the fish stay in the whale's mouth to be swallowed.

The only great whale with teeth instead of baleen is the sperm whale. It eats large squid.

PREVIOUS PAGES:
PENNANTFISH *(ALECTIS CILIARIS)* WITH TREVALLY *(CARANX* SP.), WARM OCEANS OF THE WORLD

FEEDING HUMPBACK WHALES *(MEGAPTERA NOVAEANGLIAE)*, WORLDWIDE

LEOPARD SEAL (HYDRURGA LEPTONYX), SOUTHERN OCEANS

▲ WHY ARE THERE SO MANY SEALS IN THE ANTARCTIC?

Because people killed most of the great whales, there may be more krill for seals to eat.

Antarctic seals eat a lot of krill. Even this leopard seal, which also eats penguins and other seals, eats krill. So do the great whales. But whalers killed most of the great whales during the first half of this century. Because there are far fewer whales than there used to be, there may be more food for the seals.

Today, the crabeater seal is the most abundant seal in the world. There are at least ten million of them in Antarctic waters. Despite their name, crabeater seals often eat nothing but krill.

▶ WHERE DO PENGUINS LIVE?

Only five kinds of penguins live in the Antarctic. The others live on islands and continents south of the equator.

There are seventeen kinds of penguins. Most live on islands, or on the coasts of South America, South Africa, Australia and New Zealand. One even lives on the equator, in the Galapagos Islands. There are none in the Arctic.

Penguins can't fly in the air, but they use their wings to "fly" underwater. They are very good swimmers and divers. All Antarctic penguins eat krill. Some eat almost nothing else.

The gentoo penguin eats mostly krill in the Antarctic. Farther north, where krill are less common, it eats more fish. It can dive over 50 m (150 feet) deep to catch them – as deep as a ten-story building is tall.

GENTOO PENGUIN (PYGOSCELIS PAPUA), SOUTHERN OCEANS

CRABEATER SEAL (LOBODON CARCINOPHAGUS), ANTARCTIC WATERS

WHAT ABOUT...?

Why do oil spills kill seabirds?
See page 89.

Partners

We often think of nature as a place where different kinds of animals fight or eat one another. In fact, many animals seem to get along well together. Often, one kind of animal uses another in a harmless way. Many birds in tropical America, for example, follow army ants. The army ants march through the forest by the thousands, hunting for prey. The birds catch insects that fly up to get out of the ants' way.

Other animals have become partners. They cooperate with each other in ways that help both of them. Some of these animal partners need each other so much that one or both of them would die without the other's help.

RED-BILLED OXPECKER *(BUPHAGUS ERYTHRORHYNCHUS)* ON BLACK RHINO *(DICEROS BICORNIS)*, AFRICA

CATTLE EGRET *(BUBULCUS IBIS)*, WORLDWIDE IN WARM AREAS, ON AFRICAN ELEPHANT *(LOXODONTA AFRICANA)*

▶ **WHY DO CATTLE EGRETS RIDE ON ELEPHANTS?**
These birds ride elephants, or follow them around, to catch insects the elephants stir up in the grass.

The cattle egret is a kind of heron. Instead of catching fish like many other herons, though, it follows elephants, cattle or other large animals. As these animals move through the grass, they scare grasshoppers and other insects. When the insects fly out of the way, they are easier for the egret to see and catch.

This is not a real partnership, because the egrets aren't doing anything for the elephant. They are just using it to help them find food. They will even ride on its back to get a better view of the grass.

Oxpeckers, a kind of starling, also ride on many African animals, but they may help by eating ticks that bite the animals they ride on. However, sometimes they will peck at sores and make them worse. Elephants usually will not let oxpeckers ride on them.

WHAT ABOUT...?
Why do reef fishes go to the cleaners?
See page 63.

▲ WHY DO CLOWNFISHES LIVE WITH SEA ANEMONES?
Clownfishes hide from their enemies among the stinging tentacles of a sea anemone.
Clownfishes, or anemonefishes, live on coral reefs in the Pacific and Indian oceans. A clownfish always lives with a sea anemone. If another fish chases it, it dives into the anemone's tentacles. Anemones have stinging cells on their tentacles that can kill other fishes. However, clownfishes are covered with a slime that may protect them from the anemone's sting.

We don't know if this is a real partnership. The anemone helps the clownfish, but we don't know if the clownfish helps the anemone. Some people think that it may drive off butterflyfishes that eat anemones.

BARRIER REEF CLOWNFISH (*AMPHIPRION AKINDYNOS*), REEFS OF EASTERN AUSTRALIA, NEW CALEDONIA AND THE LOYALTY ISLANDS

▼ WHY DO ANTS KEEP APHID FARMS?
Aphids are small insects that suck plant juices. They make a sugary liquid called honeydew that ants eat. In return, the ants protect the aphids.
Some ants have become aphid farmers. The ants protect the aphids from ladybugs and other enemies. Some even guard aphid eggs in their nests over the winter. In spring, they carry the babies to their food plants. In return, when an ant strokes an aphid, the aphid makes honeydew for the ant.

Aphid farming has been going on for a long time. Ants and aphids have been found together as thirty-million-year-old fossils.

ANTS (*FORMICA* SP.) TENDING APHIDS

The Temperate Forest

One of the most beautiful spectacles in the world is the changing color of autumn leaves. But it doesn't happen everywhere. In eastern North America, China and Japan, you can see the best of fall: the brilliant reds and oranges of different kinds of maple trees.

The changing colors are a sign that winter is coming. Winter tests the survival skills of the animals and plants of the temperate forest.

WHAT ABOUT...?
How do members of a wolf pack keep from fighting?
See page 41.

EASTERN PIPISTRELLE BAT *(PIPISTRELLUS SUBFLAVUS)* HIBERNATING, EASTERN NORTH AMERICA

SUGAR MAPLE *(ACER SACCHARUM)*, EASTERN NORTH AMERICA

■ WHY DO SOME MAMMALS HIBERNATE?
Hibernating is a way to save energy and survive during the winter.

Mammals need a great deal of energy to keep their body temperatures high all year round. In winter, not only is it cold, but the food that animals need for energy can also be hard to find. Some mammals, such as squirrels and bats, solve this problem by hibernating.

Hibernating is different from sleeping. A hibernating animal lowers its body temperature and slows its breathing and heartbeat. Bats, for example, may lower their temperatures from about 35°C (102°F) to slightly below 0°C (32°F). That way, they use less energy than they would if they were awake, or even asleep in the normal way. Scientists found a hibernating red bat that had a temperature of only -5°C (23°F)!

◄ HOW DO AUTUMN LEAVES CHANGE COLOR?
In autumn, the green color in a leaf disappears. Other colors in the leaf, colors that may have been there all the time, show through.

Some of the colors we see in fall leaves are there, in the leaf, all summer. We can't see them because they are hidden by the green coloring, called chlorophyll, which plants use to make food. In the autumn, leaves stop making food and the chlorophyll disappears. That lets us see the other colors.

The bright reds of maples form in a different way. Sugar builds up in their leaves in the fall. This causes the leaf to produce the red pigments that make maples so beautiful.

SNOWSHOE HARE *(LEPUS AMERICANUS)*, NORTH AMERICA, IN ITS SUMMER *(ABOVE)* AND WINTER *(BELOW)* COATS

▲ WHY DOES THE SNOWSHOE HARE CHANGE COLOR?
Snowshoe hares turn white in winter. That makes them hard to see against the snow.

In summer, the snowshoe hare is mostly dark brown. As the days grow shorter in autumn, the hare grows a new snow-white coat. Only the tips of its ears stay black. Its two coats help it to hide from bobcats, lynx and other predators.

A white coat is not the only adaptation the snowshoe hare has for survival in the winter. It gets its name from its large, hairy hind feet. Like real snowshoes, the hare's feet keep it from sinking as it runs over the deep snow.

Grasslands

EURASIAN SKYLARK *(ALAUDA ARVENSIS),* EUROPE AND NORTHERN ASIA

About 25 million years ago, the world's climate changed. Land that was once covered with forest grew too dry for many kinds of trees. The first grasses slowly moved out of the forest, and spread over vast open areas.

Animals followed the grasses out of the forest, and in time, they changed, too. Eating was a problem, because grass is hard to digest. Plant eaters, from mice to rhinoceroses, had to evolve new ways to live and eat on the grasslands. Birds even had to evolve a new way to sing.

▲ HOW DID THE SKYLARK GET ITS NAME?
Skylarks fly high into the air before they sing.

Many male birds sing to warn other birds to keep out of their territory. In the forest, a bird often sits high in a tree while it sings, to make sure that other birds can hear its song. But what does a bird do if there are no trees?

The skylark of Europe and Asia solves this problem by flying high into the sky. It hangs in the air, beating its wings, while it pours out its song. This behavior is called skylarking. Other grassland birds, like pipits and the Australian songlarks, do the same thing, probably for the same reason.

WHAT ABOUT...?
Why do zebras have stripes?
See page 81.

■ WHAT IS A PRAIRIE-DOG TOWN?
Prairie dogs are not dogs. They are ground squirrels from western North America. They live in large colonies called "towns."

Families of prairie dogs dig their burrows close to each other. They live together with other family groups in a town. The towns can be very large. One in Texas, many years ago, may have held 400 million animals.

Prairie dogs change the grasslands near their towns by the way they eat. They eat so many plants that only ones that grow quickly have a good chance of survival there. Prairie dogs also bite the tops off tall plants, perhaps to give themselves a better view as they watch for enemies.

Many cattle ranchers hated prairie dogs because they ate so much grass. They hunted them for many years, and today prairie dogs are rare in many places.

▶ WHY IS GRASS HARD TO EAT?
Grass has minerals in it that wear down teeth. It's also very hard to digest.

Grasses contain a lot of cellulose, the material that makes celery hard to chew. Grass-eating animals can't digest cellulose. They have to be able to hold grass in their bodies until microscopic creatures inside them break the cellulose down into starches and sugars. To do this, cows and antelopes have stomachs adapted as holding chambers. Horses use a pouch running like a pocket from their intestines.

Grass also contains tiny bits of silica, a hard mineral like glass. On dry grasslands, dust and grit cover many plants. All of these may wear down an animal's teeth. To solve this problem, many grassland animals have evolved large back teeth with thick, hard chewing surfaces.

AMERICAN BISON *(BISON BISON),* WESTERN NORTH AMERICA

WHAT ABOUT...?
What are "living stones"?
See page 19.

A Drink in the Desert

All life needs water. Plants and animals in the desert must find what little water there is and keep from losing it. Animals in hot deserts must stay in the shade if they can, away from the burning sun. Many come out only at night.

Some plants wait for the rare desert rains as seeds. After a storm, seeds sprout quickly and brightly colored flowers cover the desert. Animals may live through the long dry spells as eggs. When it rains in the deserts of Australia, tiny shield shrimp hatch in puddles on top of Uluru (Ayers Rock). For a few days, they swim in the desert.

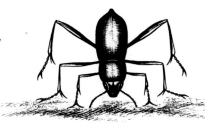

DUNE BEETLE (*ONYMACRIS UNGUICULARIS*), NAMIB DESERT, SOUTHWESTERN AFRICA

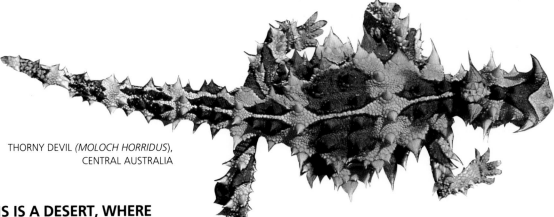

THORNY DEVIL *(MOLOCH HORRIDUS)*, CENTRAL AUSTRALIA

◄ IF THIS IS A DESERT, WHERE ARE THE CACTI?
Cacti are mostly found in North and South America. Some even grow in rainforests.
In African and Asian deserts, there are plants with thick, fleshy stems that look like cacti, but are not related to them. In Australia, the spiky clumps of spinifex grasses cover the desert.

Spinifex leaves are rolled into points to keep the sun from reaching the inside of the leaves and drying them out. Their roots grow deep into the sand to find water. Hopping mice, spinifexbirds, legless lizards and other desert animals hide in the spinifex clumps, protected from their enemies and shaded from the sun.

ULURU (AYERS ROCK), AUSTRALIA

▲ HOW DOES THE THORNY DEVIL FIND WATER?
This small, gentle lizard lives in the Australian deserts. Its sharp spines protect it from hawks and snakes. They also help it collect water.
In the morning, dew collects on the tips of the thorny devil's spikes. Tiny grooves running from the tip of each spike draw the water down through channels in its skin. When the water reaches its mouth, the lizard licks its lips to get a drink.

The thorny devil is not the only desert animal that gathers water with its body. In the Namib Desert of Africa, the dune beetle takes a bath in fog. At night, it climbs to the top of a sand dune and upends itself. Droplets of fog collect on its body and trickle down to its mouth.

■ CAN YOU FIND FROGS IN THE DESERT?
Desert frogs spend most of their lives underground. They only come out when it rains.
The desert is the last place you might expect to find a frog, but at night, after a heavy rainstorm, some desert ponds are full of calling frogs. The ponds may dry up in a few days. The frogs must mate and lay eggs, the eggs must hatch, and the tadpoles change into little frogs before the water is gone.

Then all the frogs disappear. They burrow deep underground, sometimes as much as 1 m (3 feet) down. Some, like the Australian waterholding frogs, form cocoons of skin cells that keep them from drying out in their burrows. There they wait, perhaps for years, until the next rain.

Life in the Arctic

You may think of the Arctic as a cold, empty place, but it's full of life. However, even Arctic wildlife can't do much in the winter. The plants and animals that live there have to pack a whole year of activities into the few short weeks of summer.

Then, the tundra plants bloom, clouds of insects rise from the ponds and animals from caribou to snow buntings look for food, mate and raise their young. Along the shore, flocks of seabirds and bands of seals dive for fish, and are hunted by one of the largest meat-eating animals on earth, the polar bear.

MUSKOX CIRCLE

POLAR BEARS (URSUS MARITIMUS), SHORES OF THE ARCTIC OCEAN

◄ **HOW DO POLAR BEARS KEEP WARM?**
Polar bears have thick, oily fur to keep water out and a layer of fat to keep heat in. Their fur can trap the sun's energy.
Polar bears lose almost no heat from their bodies to the Arctic cold, even when they swim through ice water. A polar bear spends a lot of time in the water. When it comes out, a few shakes get most of the water out of its oily fur. A roll in the snow is all it needs to dry off.

A polar bear's fur may keep it warm in another way, too. The hairs of a polar bear's coat are hollow. They trap ultraviolet light from the sun and carry it down to the bear's skin, where it turns into heat.

WHAT ABOUT...?
How are pussy willows pollinated?
See page 36.

▶ WHAT IS THE WORLD'S SMALLEST WILLOW?
Arctic willows are only a few centimeters (inches) tall, but may be many years old.

In warmer climates, willows may grow into tall trees. The willows of the tundra, however, are swept by Arctic winds. Instead of growing upward, they creep along the ground. Their branches weave together into a loose mat, and extra roots hold them tightly against the soil. Only their flowering branches rise into the air – perhaps up to your ankles.

ARCTIC WILLOW (*SALIX* SP.), NORTHERN NORTH AMERICA

Arctic willows may take decades to form a small mat. Like many tundra plants, they take a long time to grow. That is why the tundra is so easy to damage. Even footprints can cause damage that may take years to repair.

MUSKOXEN (*OVIBOS MOSCHATUS*), ARCTIC NORTH AMERICA AND GREENLAND

▲ WHAT ARE THE MUSKOX'S GREATEST ENEMIES?
Very cold winters, wolves and people kill muskoxen.

The muskox is not an ox. It is related to goats. Its thick coat of fine wool makes it look bigger than it is.

Winter storms that cover the ground with snow and ice can keep muskoxen from reaching the tundra plants they eat. Many may starve.

Wolves sometimes kill a calf. Muskoxen protect their young from wolves by standing around the calves in a circle, facing outwards. Unfortunately, this makes them easy for human hunters to shoot. A hundred years ago, hunters almost wiped out the muskox. Today, it is against the law to kill muskoxen, and they number in the thousands.

The Deep Sea

Far down in the depths of the sea, deeper than sunlight can reach, is the dark, cold world of the abyss. Some of the strangest creatures on earth live there. They may even look like monsters – but they are tiny monsters. Most of them could fit in the palm of your hand.

In the darkness, food can be hard to find. A deep-sea hunter may have to eat anything it runs into – even if the hunter is smaller than its meal. Finding a mate can be a problem, too. Some deep-sea fish have solved this problem in very strange ways.

▼ HOW DO DEEP-SEA ANGLERFISH KEEP A MATE?
Male anglerfish attach them-selves to a female, and stay there for the rest of their lives.
Finding a mate in the darkness of the abyss is so hard that once a male and female meet, it's a good idea for them to stick together. Deep-sea anglerfish really do.

When a male finds the much larger female, he grabs her with his teeth and holds on. Slowly, his blood vessels join with hers, and his mouth, eyes and stomach almost disappear. For the rest of his life he lives as little more than a part of her body, getting all his food through her blood.

■ WHAT FISH CAN SWALLOW OTHER FISH TWICE ITS OWN SIZE?
The black swallower can stretch its jaws and stomach wide enough to swallow fish twice its own size.
Several deep-sea fishes can swallow prey larger than themselves. What is more, they swallow them whole!

Black swallowers, gulper eels and other deep-sea hunters have huge jaws that can swing down and spread apart to make room for a large meal. Their stomachs can stretch tremendously to hold their victims. Long, needle-sharp teeth hold struggling prey and help stuff it down.

■ WHY DO DEEP-SEA CREATURES WEAR LIGHTS?
Many deep-sea animals can glow in the dark. Lights may help attract prey or a mate. They may also confuse enemies.
Many deep-sea fishes, squid, shrimp, jellyfish and other animals can light up parts of their bodies. We don't know why many of them wear lights. Some deep-sea anglerfish have lights around their mouths that may attract curious prey. Others, like the flashlight fish, seem to signal to each other with flashing lights.

Some deep-sea squids can let off a cloud of "ink" that glows bright blue in the dark. Animals chasing a squid may attack the cloud while the squid itself gets away.

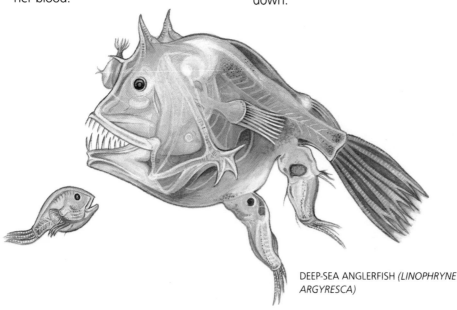

DEEP-SEA ANGLERFISH (LINOPHRYNE ARGYRESCA)

> **WHAT ABOUT...?**
> **How can seals stay underwater for so long?**
> See page 15.

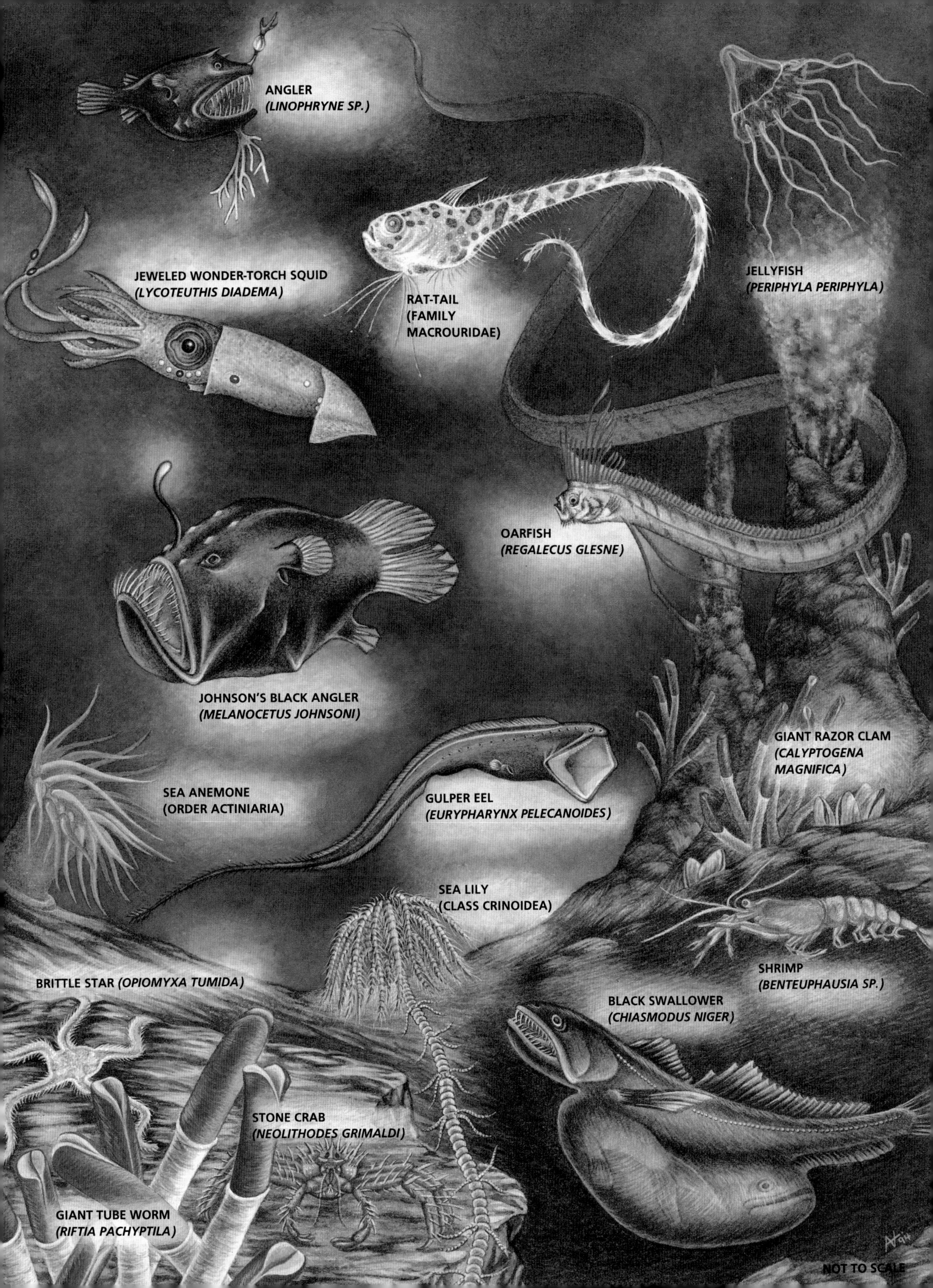

ANGLER
(*LINOPHRYNE SP.*)

JEWELED WONDER-TORCH SQUID
(*LYCOTEUTHIS DIADEMA*)

RAT-TAIL
(FAMILY
MACROURIDAE)

JELLYFISH
(*PERIPHYLA PERIPHYLA*)

OARFISH
(*REGALECUS GLESNE*)

JOHNSON'S BLACK ANGLER
(*MELANOCETUS JOHNSONI*)

GIANT RAZOR CLAM
(*CALYPTOGENA
MAGNIFICA*)

SEA ANEMONE
(ORDER ACTINIARIA)

GULPER EEL
(*EURYPHARYNX PELECANOIDES*)

SEA LILY
(CLASS CRINOIDEA)

BRITTLE STAR (*OPIOMYXA TUMIDA*)

SHRIMP
(*BENTEUPHAUSIA SP.*)

BLACK SWALLOWER
(*CHIASMODUS NIGER*)

STONE CRAB
(*NEOLITHODES GRIMALDI*)

GIANT TUBE WORM
(*RIFTIA PACHYPTILA*)

NOT TO SCALE

The Coral Reef

There is nothing more beautiful than a coral reef. Only a tropical rainforest can match a reef for the color and variety of its animal life.

Like rainforests, reefs around the world are in danger. Pollution can kill coral polyps. In some areas, people mine coral to make building material, or take shells and coral to sell to tourists. In the Philippines, some people poison the reef with cyanide to catch fish to sell to pet stores. Fishes that get only a little cyanide don't die, but they are weak enough to be caught. We have a lot of work to do if we want to save our coral reefs.

ORANGE TUBE CORAL

RED SOFT CORALS (CLASS ALCYONARIA) AND YELLOW FEATHER STARS (CLASS CRINOIDEA) ON A CORAL REEF, AUSTRALIA

■ **WHY DO CORAL REEFS NEED SUNLIGHT?**
Tiny algae live in the bodies of coral polyps. They make food for themselves and the polyps. Like other plants, algae use sunlight to make food.
If the water around the reef becomes muddy or dirty, sunlight can't reach the algae. If the algae can't make food, they and the corals will die.

When people cut down rainforests near reefs, there are no trees left to hold the soil with their roots. Rain can wash the soil out to sea. The mud and silt may kill the corals on the reef. That is why protecting rainforests protects coral reefs, too.

WHAT ABOUT...?
What are coral polyps?
See page 43.

▶ WHY DO REEF FISHES GO TO THE CLEANERS?

Tiny animals called parasites ride on reef fishes, like fleas on a dog. They can make the fishes sick. Reef fishes visit cleaning stations where small fishes or shrimp can remove their parasites.

Just beside the eye of this spotted sweetlips is another, much smaller fish – a cleaner wrasse. The sweetlips has visited the wrasse at its cleaning station. The wrasse is checking it for parasites and will eat any it finds. The sweetlips holds very still so that the wrasse can even clean inside its mouth.

Cleaner wrasses, other cleaning fish and cleaner shrimp are very important parts of the reef community. If there are no cleaners, parasites may make the other fish so sick that many will die.

MANY-SPOTTED SWEETLIPS *(PLECTORHYNCHUS CHAETODONOIDES)* AND CLEANER WRASSE *(LABROIDES DIMIDIATUS)*, TROPICAL PACIFIC AND INDIAN OCEANS

CROWN-OF-THORNS STARFISH *(ACANTHASTER PLANCI)*, RED SEA, INDIAN AND WEST PACIFIC OCEANS

▲ WHAT DOES THE CROWN-OF-THORNS STARFISH DO TO REEFS?

The crown-of-thorns starfish eats coral polyps. Large numbers of them can damage a reef.

The crown-of-thorns starfish eats by pushing its stomach out through its mouth and over its food. Its diges- tive juices turn coral polyps into a soup the starfish can absorb.

Sometimes large numbers of these starfish attack a reef and kill much of its coral. Given time, the coral will grow back. Lately, how- ever, starfish attacks have happened more often. Some scientists think that people have somehow made this happen. Fishermen may have caught too many of the fishes that eat the crown-of-thorns. With fewer predators, there may be more starfish.

HOW CAN I HELP PROTECT CORAL REEFS?

One way is not to buy coral or shell souvenirs and jewelry. If you have a marine aquarium, make sure the fish you buy for it were caught with nets, not cyanide. If you are lucky enough to visit a reef, remember how easy it is to damage it. Don't touch live corals – even a light touch can kill the polyps. (It's a good idea not to touch any live animal on the reef. Some of them can give you a nasty sting!)

Mountains

Climbing a high mountain is like taking a trip into the Arctic or the Antarctic. As you climb, the air grows colder. Trees grow shorter, until at the tree line they disappear altogether.

Above the tree line is the world of the alpine tundra, where animals and plants must adapt to wind and cold. For those who can survive there, the mountaintops provide a home that they don't have to share with their less-hardy cousins.

▼ WHY DON'T MOUNTAIN GOATS FALL OFF NARROW MOUNTAIN LEDGES?
Mountain goats have feet made for climbing on rock.
The American mountain goat is one of the most sure-footed of animals. The rim of its hoof is stiff, to take the wear and tear of mountain climbing. In the center of its hoof is a bumpy pad that grips the rocks and helps put spring into the mountain goat's leaps. The hoof can even act like a suction cup, clamping on to the rocks. A dew claw, a small outer toe above the hoof, also helps the animal hold on to steep slopes.

With this equipment, a mountain goat can move along narrow ledges, climb nearly vertical cliffs, and jump easily from rock to rock.

MOUNTAIN GOAT HOOF

MOUNTAIN GOAT *(OREAMNOS AMERICANUS)*, WESTERN NORTH AMERICA

WHAT ABOUT...?
Have animals always lived where they are today?
See page 72.

▲ HOW DOES THE PIKA PREPARE FOR WINTER?
Pikas dry piles of hay in the sun. They store their hay as food for the winter.

Pikas look something like guinea pigs, but they are really short-eared relatives of rabbits. The American pika lives among piles of rocks high in the mountains of western North America.

Pikas remain active during the cold mountain winters, when there are few fresh plants to eat. During the summer, they cut hay from the mountain meadows and dry it in the sun. When the hay is dry, they store it away, and guard it from other

AMERICAN PIKA *(OCHOTONA PRINCEPS)* GATHERING HAY, WESTERN NORTH AMERICA

pikas who might try to steal it. Their stores of hay provide them with enough food to survive the winter.

▶ HOW DO ALPINE PLANTS SURVIVE?
Mountain plants can protect themselves against cold winds and intense sunlight.

Above the tree line, plants may be tiny, with flowers almost as big as the rest of the plant. They grow in mats, hugging the rocks for protection from harsh winds.

The dry air and strong sunlight of the heights can also harm the plants by drying them out. Many alpine plants are covered with silky hairs that protect their leaves from the wind and reflect sunlight away.

DWARF MONKSHOOD *(ACONITUM SP.),* WESTERN NORTH AMERICA

Others coat their leaves with wax. This keeps water in.

Tropical mountaintops are harsh places to live, too. Without winter, though, plants can grow all year.

Tropical alpine plants are not dwarfs like this monkshood. Some may be taller than a grown person.

Rainforests

More animals and plants live in tropical rainforests than anywhere else. A temperate forest may have only a dozen different kinds of trees, but a tropical rainforest may have hundreds. Scientists are still discovering new rainforest animals. Two new kinds of rainforest monkey were found in Brazil in the 1980s.

But the rainforest is in danger. Around the world, an area of rainforest the size of fifty-seven football fields is destroyed every minute. Nineteen million rainforest trees are cut down every day. Saving the rainforest is one of the most important things we can do to help our planet.

RIO MAUÉS MARMOSET
(CALLITHRIX MAUESI),
DISCOVERED IN BRAZIL IN 1992

WHAT ABOUT...?
Do coral reefs need rainforests?
See page 62.

◄ **WHY ARE RAINFOREST PLANTS SO IMPORTANT FOR PEOPLE?**
The people of the rainforest use the plants around them for food, clothing, tools and medicine.
Because rainforest plants are attacked by so many insects and diseases, they have evolved hundreds of kinds of poisons and other chemical defenses. Many of these kill germs that cause human diseases like malaria. Others can ease pain or stop bleeding.

The chemicals in the rainforest can be used for more than just medicine. Natural rubber comes from the sap of a rainforest tree. The sap of another tree can run a diesel engine. As rainforest plants, and the rainforest peoples that understand them, disappear, we are losing the treasures of the forest.

AMAZON RAINFOREST, BRAZIL

▶ WHY DO RAINFOREST TREES HAVE ROOTS ABOVE GROUND?

Rainforest soils are very shallow. Trees need roots above ground to hold themselves up.

In a temperate forest, the soils are rich and deep. Trees send their roots far into the ground. But in tropical rainforests, soils are often poor and shallow. There is no food for the trees deep underground, so they send their roots out along the surface. They take minerals from rotting leaves on the forest floor.

Without deep roots, trees need something to keep from falling over. Many rainforest trees have prop roots, or broad sail-like supports called buttresses, growing out from the trunk, to hold themselves up. One rainforest palm even uses prop roots to "push" itself up again if another tree falls and knocks it over.

STEM ROOTS ON A RAINFOREST TREE, COSTA RICA.

HOW CAN I HELP SAVE THE RAINFORESTS?

In the mountains of Costa Rica, there is a rainforest that has been saved entirely by children.

It's called the Children's Eternal Forest, and it covers over 13 000 ha (32,000 acres). Thousands of children all over the world have helped raise money to buy the land, so that no one may cut down the trees.

There is still more forest to buy there, and your class can help raise the money to save it. Ask your teacher to write to The Children's Rainforest, P.O. Box 936, Lewiston, Maine, USA 04240.

▶ WHY DO SO MANY RAINFOREST SNAKES LIVE IN TREES?

Many rainforest snakes eat lizards, frogs, birds and other animals that live in the tree-tops.

Snakes can't chase an animal that flies or leaps to another branch. Some snakes, like this emerald tree boa, wait patiently for their prey. Their green skin makes it hard for their prey to see them among the leaves.

Tree vipers have fast-acting poisons that paralyze a victim before it can hop out of reach. The blunt-headed tree snake has a special spine, with bones that lock together like the links on a bicycle chain. Its spine lets it reach far out into the air to snatch a lizard from its perch.

EMERALD TREE BOA *(CORALLUS CANINA)*, SOUTH AMERICA

Millions of Insects

High in the treetops of the tropical rainforest is the insect capital of the world. There may be more kinds of insects living there than in all the rest of the planet put together. The number of species in a rainforest can be mind-boggling. The top of one tree in Peru, for example, had fifty-four kinds of ants – more than in the entire British Isles.

Today, the insects, and their homes, are in danger. Insect species are disappearing every day as tropical rainforests are burned or cut down. Most of them have never been studied, or even named, by scientists, but that doesn't make them less important.

▼ **WHAT IS THE LARGEST LIVING BUTTERFLY?**
The female Queen Alexandra's birdwing from New Guinea.
This butterfly measures 28 cm (11 inches) across. Its wings would reach from the top of this page to the bottom.

QUEEN ALEXANDRA'S BIRDWING
(ORNITHOPTERA ALEXANDRAE), NEW GUINEA

ANT *(ECTATOMMA* SP.*), AMAZON RAINFOREST, SOUTH AMERICA

▼ WHY DO SOME INSECTS WEAR DISGUISES?
This caterpillar looks and acts like a snake. Its disguise may scare its enemies away.

This may look like a snake, but it's really a caterpillar. Those big "eyes" aren't eyes, just colored spots. They aren't even on its head, but on the middle of its body.

When it's attacked, the caterpillar swings back and forth like a snake. It may even pretend to strike. To look more frightening, it pumps liquid to its false "eyes," swelling them up so they seem to "open."

This disguise may scare away birds and other animals that would like to eat the caterpillar. Many rainforest insects look and act like more dangerous animals for the same reason. Others look like leaves, bits of bark or even bird droppings. Disguises like these help them hide from their enemies, as long as they hold still.

Hunters may wear disguises, too. Some mantises, for example, look like pink flowers. Any insect that comes looking for nectar is caught and eaten.

■ WHY ARE THERE SO MANY KINDS OF RAINFOREST INSECTS?
The rainforest has more kinds of homes where different insects can live than any other place on earth.

A rainforest may have hundreds of kinds of huge trees. Each tree is like a giant apartment building, with many different kinds of "apart-ments" where insects can live. These include leaves, branches, stems and even vines, orchids and other plants that grow on the tree.

Because there is so much for insects to eat in the rainforest, each kind of insect can spend its whole life in its own "apartment" without running out of food. The top of each tree, where the sun shines, may have different insects from the darker lower branches, the trunk or the forest floor. All of these plant-eaters themselves provide food for thou-sands of meat-eating insect species.

SNAKE CATERPILLAR (FAMILY SPHINGIDAE), AMAZON RAINFOREST, SOUTH AMERICA

WHAT ABOUT...?
Why are some butterfly wings so colorful?
See page 22.

Animal Travelers

For hundreds of years people wondered where the birds went in the winter. The Romans thought that swallows buried themselves in the mud. Now we know that birds, and many other kinds of animals, from fishes to whales and from butterflies to elephants, migrate.

They travel long distances every year, finding their way as accurately as if they had compasses and road maps. Even the dinosaurs may have migrated, millions of years ago.

ARCTIC TERN *(STERNA PARADISAEA),* BREEDS ARCTIC, WINTERS ANTARCTICA

SOCKEYE SALMON *(ONCORHYNCHUS NERKA),* NORTH PACIFIC COASTLINES

▲ HOW DOES A SALMON FIND THE PLACE WHERE IT WAS BORN?

Salmon live at sea, but lay their eggs in fresh water, in the same streams where they themselves were born. They find their nesting grounds by smell.

We don't know how salmon find the right rivers to swim into from the ocean. But once in fresh water, they can tell which way to swim by the odor of each stream that flows into the river. They follow the smell into smaller and smaller streams. They leap waterfalls and force their way past anything that tries to stop them, until they reach the spot where they were born.

Atlantic salmon return to their birthplace several times. But Pacific salmon, like these sockeyes, lay their eggs only once. Worn out by their journey, they die after spawning.

▼ HOW DO WE KNOW WHERE MONARCH BUTTERFLIES GO?

A scientist put tags with numbers on the wings of some monarchs. When people caught the tagged butterflies, he could tell how far they had flown.

A Canadian scientist named Fred Urquhart wanted to find out where monarch butterflies spend the winter. He and his helpers caught monarchs, put special tags on their wings and let them go. Anyone who found a tagged butterfly was asked to write to the address on the tag.

By marking the places where the tags were found on a map, Dr. Urquhart could trace the butterflies' journeys. He followed the direction they were going, and he was able to discover their wintering ground. It's a fir forest in Mexico, where the butterflies cover the trees by the thousands.

TAGGED MONARCH OR WANDERER BUTTERFLY *(DANAUS PLEXIPPUS),* NORTH AMERICA, PACIFIC ISLANDS AND AUSTRALIA

WHAT ABOUT...?
How do animals and plants survive in the Arctic?
See pages 58-59.

▲ **WHY DO BIRDS MIGRATE?**
Birds migrate to find winter food.

They don't migrate to escape the cold. If birds can find the right food, they will stay where they are, or not fly as far. These snow geese fly from the Arctic to the southern United States. Other Arctic birds, such as the Arctic tern, fly almost to the Antarctic.

Why fly back to the Arctic again? In summer, there is lots of food in the Arctic for young birds, and not as many other kinds of birds to share it with. For snow geese, this makes it a better place to nest.

MIGRATING SNOW GEESE (*ANSER CAERULESCENS*), NORTH AMERICA AND EASTERN ASIA

The Geography of Life

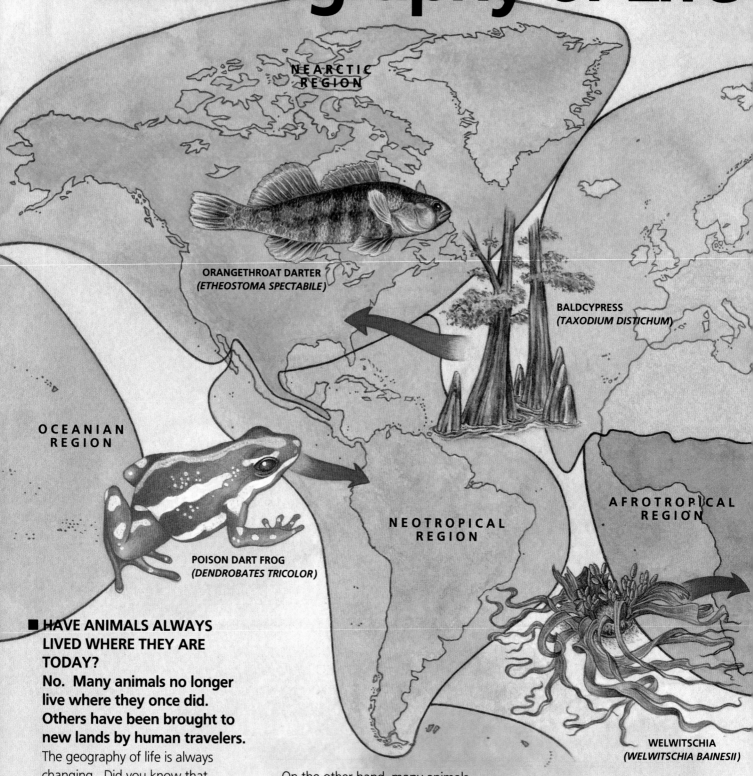

NEARCTIC REGION

ORANGETHROAT DARTER
(ETHEOSTOMA SPECTABILE)

BALDCYPRESS
(TAXODIUM DISTICHUM)

OCEANIAN REGION

POISON DART FROG
(DENDROBATES TRICOLOR)

NEOTROPICAL REGION

AFROTROPICAL REGION

WELWITSCHIA
(WELWITSCHIA BAINESII)

■ HAVE ANIMALS ALWAYS LIVED WHERE THEY ARE TODAY?

No. Many animals no longer live where they once did. Others have been brought to new lands by human travelers.

The geography of life is always changing. Did you know that elephants and camels once lived in North America? Camels may have evolved there, too. There were once rhinoceroses in Europe, giraffes in Asia and flamingos in Australia.

On the other hand, many animals and plants now live in places far from their natural homes, because humans have brought them there. Sometimes they become pests in their new homes. Mosquitoes in Hawaii, mongooses in Jamaica, rabbits and foxes in Australia, and Nile perch in African lakes have endangered or even destroyed native wildlife.

Pandas and peacocks live in Asia, koalas and kookaburras in Australia, hippos and hartebeest in Africa, macaws and marmosets in South America. In fact, each part of the world has its own special plants and animals. Over a century ago, Alfred Russell Wallace noticed this and divided the world into biogeographic regions. Today, the study of biogeography – the geography of life – helps us to understand how animals and plants evolved and spread over the globe.

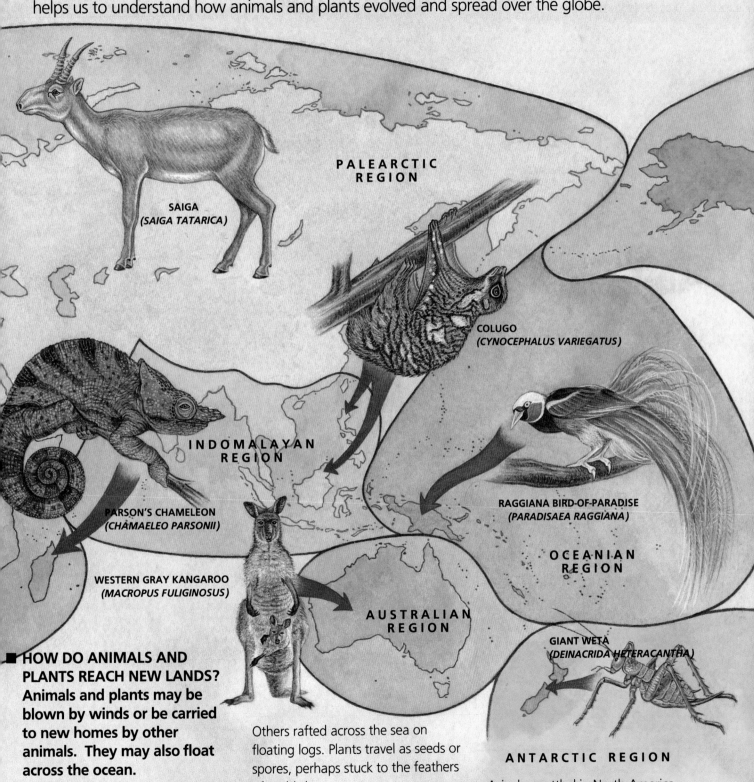

PALEARCTIC REGION

SAIGA
(SAIGA TATARICA)

COLUGO
(CYNOCEPHALUS VARIEGATUS)

INDOMALAYAN REGION

RAGGIANA BIRD-OF-PARADISE
(PARADISAEA RAGGIANA)

PARSON'S CHAMELEON
(CHAMAELEO PARSONII)

OCEANIAN REGION

WESTERN GRAY KANGAROO
(MACROPUS FULIGINOSUS)

AUSTRALIAN REGION

GIANT WETA
(DEINACRIDA HETERACANTHA)

ANTARCTIC REGION

■ **HOW DO ANIMALS AND PLANTS REACH NEW LANDS? Animals and plants may be blown by winds or be carried to new homes by other animals. They may also float across the ocean.**
Once all the continents were joined together. Some animals and plants spread from one place to another before the continents drifted apart.

Others rafted across the sea on floating logs. Plants travel as seeds or spores, perhaps stuck to the feathers of seabirds.

Birds and insects still fly to new homes. The cattle egret, a bird once found only in Africa and tropical

Asia, has settled in North America, South America and Australia within the past one hundred years. It's now found almost around the world.

North America

North America was once a wildlife paradise. Millions of bison covered the plains, and billions of passenger pigeons – the most abundant bird in the world – darkened the skies as they passed. People hunted them, believing that they would last forever. Today, there are only a few thousand bison left, and the passenger pigeon is extinct.

But North America is still full of wild creatures, from colorful warblers to alligators. The largest trees in the world, the redwoods, grow in California, and in the east the maple woodlands provide the finest show of fall colors in the world.

PASSENGER PIGEON *(ECTOPISTES MIGRATORIUS)*, EASTERN NORTH AMERICA (EXTINCT)

GRAY FOX *(UROCYON CINEREOARGENTEUS)*, NORTH AMERICA TO NORTHERN SOUTH AMERICA

WHAT ABOUT...?
Why do antelopes have horns?
See page 20.

▲ CAN FOXES CLIMB TREES?
The gray fox can. Sometimes it even makes a den in a hollow tree.
Most members of the dog family can't climb, but the graceful gray fox is good at it. It can shinny up a tree trunk and leap from branch to branch. It often climbs trees if it is being chased.

Gray foxes make dens to rest in or to give birth to their babies. Gray fox dens are usually burrows in the ground like those of other foxes, but they may make them in a hollow tree, too. One gray fox's den in a tree was over 9 m (29 feet) up.

VIRGINIA OPOSSUM *(DIDELPHIS VIRGINIANA)*, SOUTHERN CANADA TO COSTA RICA

▶ DO KANGAROOS HAVE AMERICAN COUSINS?

Opossums carry their babies in a pouch, like their cousins the kangaroos, but they live in the Americas, not in Australia.

When we think about marsupials – animals with pouches – we usually think of Australia, home of the kangaroo. But the opossums of the Americas are marsupials, too. Newborn opossums, the size of bumblebees, crawl to their mother's pouch to nurse and grow.

The Virginia opossum arrived in North America from South America during the last ice age. Opossums will eat almost anything, including human garbage, and have done well in our farms and cities. They have spread through much of the United States and reached Canada only about 140 years ago.

■ WHAT IS AN AXOLOTL?

An axolotl is a salamander that never grows up. It can breed, but it looks like a larva all its life.

Tiger salamanders and their relatives are amphibians, like frogs. They lay their eggs in ponds. Their babies, or larvae, stay there until they are grown, breathing through feathery gills.

A Mexican cousin of the tiger salamander never becomes a land animal. Axolotls keep their gills and tail fins, and stay in the water all their lives.

In places like Texas and Oklahoma, USA, tiger salamander larvae don't always turn into land-living adults. Some stay in the water like axolotls. They may do this because the land where they live is too dry or hot for them.

PRONGHORN *(ANTILOCAPRA AMERICANA)*, WESTERN NORTH AMERICA

◀ WHEN IS AN ANTELOPE NOT AN ANTELOPE?

When it's a pronghorn! The pronghorn "antelope" is the only living member of its family.

The pronghorn of the American plains is often called an antelope. In fact, it is the last living member of a special family of North American hoofed animals called antilocaprids. The pronghorn is the only horned mammal that sheds its horn sheath every year. Some of its fossil relatives were bizarre-looking. One had six horns!

The pronghorn is one of the fastest animals in the world. It can run as fast as 98 km/h (61 mph). Speed is its only defense against coyotes and bobcats.

South America

Tropical America has more birds, more butterflies and more freshwater fishes than anywhere else in the world. Most of them live in the world's largest rainforest, which grows along the world's largest river, the Amazon. Even its fishes may live in flooded rainforests, swimming among the trees to feed on fallen fruits.

Not all of South America is in the tropics, though. Its southern end reaches towards Antarctica. The south may not have as many kinds of animals or plants as the rainforest, but places like Argentina's Peninsula Valdés have huge colonies of seals and penguins.

TAMBAQI (*COLOSSOMA MACROPOMUM*), A FRUIT-EATING FISH OF THE AMAZON

▶ **WHY DO SLOTHS HAVE GREEN FUR IN THE RAINY SEASON? Sloth fur looks green because tiny plants grow on it. The color makes it harder for the sloth's enemies to see it.**

A sloth is a living pot for plants. Blue-green algae live in special grooves on each hair of its long, coarse outer coat. In the rainy season, the sloth's fur turns greenish as the algae grow. This camouflage makes it hard for predators to spot it among the treetops. Sloths sometimes eat the algae by licking their fur.

Sloths are wonderfully adapted for eating forest leaves. They have huge stomachs that may hold tough leaves for a month while they digest. Even their slowness helps. Leaves don't provide much food energy, so sloths move as little as possible to save what energy they have.

HOFFMANN'S TWO-TOED SLOTH (*CHOLOEPUS HOFFMANNI*), CENTRAL AND NORTHERN SOUTH AMERICA

▼ WHY DOES THE TOUCAN HAVE SUCH A BIG BILL?
The toucan's long bill lets it pick and eat many kinds of fruits.

In the tropics, animals can eat fruit all year long. Toucans and other birds have special adaptations for fruit-eating. A toucan's bill can reach out like a long arm to pick hard-to-reach fruits, and can open wide to hold large ones. It can also catch lizards or pluck baby birds from their nests.

The toucan's bill may have other uses, too. It may be big enough to scare off small hawks. Its bright colors may help different kinds of toucans tell each other apart; each species has a different pattern.

WHAT ABOUT...?
Why are tropical American poison dart frogs so colorful?
See page 28.

KEEL-BILLED TOUCAN *(RAMPHASTOS SULFURATUS)*, MEXICO TO VENEZUELA

MARGAY *(FELIS WIEDII)*, MEXICO TO ARGENTINA

◄ WHICH CATS ARE THE BEST TREE-CLIMBERS?
The little margay of tropical America and the clouded leopard of Southeast Asia are the best tree-climbers. They can run down a trunk head first.

All cats can climb trees, though some, like the cheetah, aren't very good at it. The margay spends most of its time in trees. It can turn its ankle joints completely around so that its feet point backwards. That lets it hang onto and run down a tree trunk upside down. Your pet cat can't do that!

Unfortunately, so many margays have been hunted for their fur that they have become rare in many areas. It takes fifteen margays to make one fur coat! Today, it is against the law to take margay furs to other countries to sell.

Europe and Asia

The largest wildlife region on our planet stretches from Europe and North Africa across most of Asia to China and Japan. It holds the world's largest forest, highest mountains and deepest lake.

Some of the wildlife of Eurasia has become familiar around the world, because Europeans carried it with them wherever they went. The ancestors of many domestic animals and many farm crops and weeds came from Eurasia. So did the rats, mice, starlings and pigeons that share our cities with us. But though some Eurasian animals have spread throughout the world, others are on the edge of extinction.

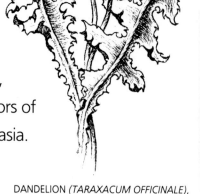

DANDELION *(TARAXACUM OFFICINALE)*, ORIGINALLY EUROPE

CAN I GROW WILD TULIPS?

You can buy the bulbs of several kinds of wild tulips at a good gardening store.

They are usually called "species" tulips by gardeners. Most species tulips bloom earlier than the commoner hybrid tulips, and look very pretty in a garden.

Sadly, too many plant bulbs are being taken from the wild. Some kinds are becoming rare. Make sure your plants were grown in a nursery!

▼ WHERE DO TULIPS COME FROM?

Most wild tulips grow in the mountains of central Asia. They are much smaller than the tulips we grow in gardens.

The tulips in our gardens have ancestors that you might not recognize. Wild tulips are not much bigger than a crocus. There are many kinds in the mountains of central Asia. They have red, yellow, pink or white flowers.

The mountains have cold, wet winters and hot, dry summers. By storing food in bulbs underground over the winter, wild tulips are ready to grow quickly during the very short spring. Soon after the snow melts, the mountain meadows may be covered with their flowers.

WILD TULIPS *(TULIPA SP.),* CENTRAL ASIA

► WHY IS THE GIANT PANDA SO RARE?

Giant pandas need forests of bamboo. There are not many places left for pandas to live.

There are only about 1000 giant pandas left in China. Pandas need forests of their favorite food, bamboo. Once these forests covered huge areas. Today, only tiny patches remain, each with a few pandas. Because these wooded areas are far apart, the pandas can't meet others of their kind to mate. As their homes disappear, the pandas die. Some pandas are still being shot for their skins, although this is against the law.

Everybody loves pandas, and many zoos would like to have them. Unfortunately, pandas do not often have babies in zoos. The best way to save pandas may be to leave them alone and to stop cutting down their forest homes.

GIANT PANDA *(AILUROPODA MELANOLEUCA)*, WESTERN CHINA

WESTERN HEDGEHOG *(ERINACEUS EUROPAEUS)*, EUROPE

◄ HOW DOES A HEDGEHOG ROLL INTO A BALL?

Hedgehogs have a special skin muscle that acts like the drawstring on a bag.

A hedgehog wears an armor of about 5000 sharp spines, but its belly is not protected. If it is attacked, though, it can roll into a spiky ball.

When the hedgehog starts to roll up, the loose skin on its back slides down over its head and rump. Then a strong ring of muscle around the edge of its back skin contracts, like the drawstring on a bag. This pulls the skin together over the hedgehog's belly and legs, closing the "bag." As its skin gets tighter, tiny muscles pull the hedgehog's spines up, making the animal even spikier than before.

WHAT ABOUT...?
How do animals use people?
See pages 90-91.

Tropical Africa

Only a few thousand years ago, large animals of all kinds roamed on every continent. Today, only in Africa can you see what the world must have been like then. Herds of elephants, giraffes, zebras, antelopes and other animals still wander the plains, and great hunters like the lion stalk them through the grass.

Even in Africa, though, wildlife is disappearing, thanks to an animal that evolved there and spread throughout the world. That animal, of course, is man. It's up to us to see that the greatest wildlife spectacle left in the world doesn't vanish.

LION *(PANTHERA LEO)*, AFRICA AND NORTHWESTERN INDIA

▼ HOW DO ELEPHANTS TAKE CARE OF THEIR BABIES?
Elephant babies are cared for by their mother, sisters and aunts.
Baby African elephants live in herds. Their mother, older sisters, aunts and cousins all help to take care of them.

AFRICAN ELEPHANT *(LOXODONTA AFRICANA)*, AFRICA

They take ten to thirteen years to grow up.

Each herd is led by an old female elephant, the matriarch. When male babies grow up, the matriarch drives them out of the herd. From then on they live alone, or with a few other males in a bachelor herd.

HOW CAN I HELP SAVE ELEPHANTS?
You can become an ELEFRIEND. Write to ELEFRIENDS, Cherry Tree Cottage, Coldharbour, Dorking, Surrey RH5 6HA, United Kingdom, for information on how you can help make your home, your school or your city into ELEFRIENDLY ZONES. You may even be able to adopt an elephant family!

GIRAFFE
(*GIRAFFA CAMELOPARDALIS*),
AFRICA SOUTH OF THE SAHARA

WHAT ABOUT...?
Why do monkeys take so long to grow up?
See page 39.

◄ HOW DO GIRAFFES USE THEIR NECKS?

Giraffes use their necks to reach their food. They also use them to fight each other.

The giraffe is the tallest animal in the world. A male giraffe can stand 5.5 m (18 feet) high, three times the height of a tall man. Its long neck helps it get to leaves other animals can't reach. Male giraffes stretch up for the highest leaves, but females usually eat leaves growing lower down. That way there is enough food for everyone.

Young male giraffes also use their necks for a special kind of fighting called necking. They swing their necks like swords, trying to hit each other with their heads.

Strangely enough, a giraffe has the same number of neck bones – seven – as you do.

■ WHY DO ZEBRAS HAVE STRIPES?

Zebras usually live together in large herds, sometimes with hundreds of animals. A zebra's stripes may be a way of letting other zebras know it is part of the herd.

Some scientists think that the zebra's stripes act as a signal to other zebras. They have found that zebras seem to like to stand near striped things – even signs with stripes painted on them. Perhaps the stripes make them feel comfortable. That may be why zebras in a herd stay together without fighting. The stripes might send the message "You can stay near me. I won't hurt you."

The stripes may also confuse hunters. When the herd runs away, the stripes may make it hard for lions and other predators to tell one zebra from another.

Southeast Asia

Gliding snakes, climbing turtles, hairy rhinoceroses, insect-eating vines – you can find them all in the rainforests of tropical Asia. Along its muddy seashores are fishes that spend more time out of the water than in it, and a giant seagoing crocodile that includes people in its diet. This region's thousands of islands have special creatures of their own. Among them is one of our own closest relatives, the orangutan, and the Komodo dragon, at 3 m (10 feet) the world's largest lizard.

KOMODO DRAGON *(VARANUS KOMODOENSIS)*, KOMODO ISLAND, INDONESIA

Southeast Asia is one of the richest wildlife regions in the world, and, sadly, one of the most endangered.

HOW CAN I HELP SAVE THE TIGER?

Your school can join "The Tiger Troops." Besides helping to save tigers, you will have a chance to play games, enter painting contests and receive the latest news about tigers. Ask your teacher to write to The Tiger Trust, Ousden, Newmarket, Suffolk, CB8 8TN, United Kingdom.

◄ WHY ARE TIGERS IN DANGER?
There are only about 4700 wild tigers left. People still hunt them for their bones, which are used as medicine.

Tigers once lived from Turkey to Siberia. People took over much of the tiger's land, and hunting wiped them out of many areas. Tigers are now extinct in many Asian countries. Forests where tigers live are still being cut down.

Today, more tigers than ever are being killed by poachers. The poachers sell their bones to people in China who use them as a medicine. Conservationists are looking for ways to save the tiger's forests, and to persuade people not to use tiger bone.

TIGER *(PANTHERA TIGRIS)*, SOUTHERN AND EASTERN ASIA

WHAT ABOUT...?
How do Asian pitcher plants eat insects?
See page 33.

HARLEQUIN FLYING FROG
(RHACOPHORUS PARDALIS),
BORNEO

▲ DO FLYING FROGS FLY?

Flying frogs don't really fly. They glide from tree to tree, using their long webbed toes as a parachute.

Most frogs use their webbed feet for swimming, but not the flying frogs. They live in the high branches of rainforest trees. If they are chased by a predator, they can launch themselves into space, spread their toes and glide to safety.

Frogs aren't the only gliders in Southeast Asian forests. "Flying" snakes flatten themselves out like ribbons and leap from high limbs. "Flying" dragon lizards, with long ribs that support a pair of sails, dart from tree to tree like paper airplanes. Giant "flying" squirrels, the size of a toy kite, float through the air for 100 m (300 feet).

A strange gliding mammal, the colugo, has a sheet of skin that stretches from its neck to the tips of its fingers and toes, and on to the tip of its tail. The size of a cat, it is almost helpless on the ground.

▼ WHAT IS THE WORLD'S LARGEST FLOWER?

The flowers of a rafflesia can be up to a meter (yard) across. They smell like rotting meat.

In the mountain forests of Southeast Asia live the rare rafflesia plants. When they aren't flowering, you can't even see them. Their bodies are only strands of tissue that live inside certain vines and steal food from them.

Their flowers, though, are amazing. Great round buds grow for months to the size of pumpkins. Then they open – for only a week – revealing the world's largest flowers. The smaller kinds are the size of dinner plates, but the largest ones could fill a shopping cart and may weigh 7 kg (15 pounds).

Some kinds of rafflesia flowers have no smell. Others stink like rotten meat, attracting the flies that pollinate them.

RAFFLESIA *(RAFFLESIA ARNOLDI)*, SUMATRA

Australia

Many animal groups common in other lands are missing in Australia, and many of its own animals and plants are found nowhere else. They include the platypus and echidna, the only mammals that lay eggs; the gastric-brooding frogs that swallow their young and hold them in their stomachs; *Rhizanthella*, an orchid that flowers underground; and the satin bowerbird, whose male attracts females by building an avenue of twigs and painting it with crushed berries. Millions of years as an island has meant that life in Australia has evolved in its own, special way.

PLATYPUS *(ORNITHORHYNCHUS ANATINUS)*, EASTERN AUSTRALIA

▼ WHERE IS "THE LAND OF PARROTS"?
Australia was once called "Terra Psittacorum" – The Land of Parrots. Over fifty kinds of parrots live there.
Parrots are everywhere in Australia. The colorful rainbow lorikeet and its relatives eat pollen from the flowering trees. Noisy flocks of white and pink cockatoos fly over the central deserts. Some parrots take the place of woodpeckers, which do not live in Australia. They can't peck at bark, but they tear it up with their powerful bills, hunting for grubs.

You may even own an Australian parrot. The budgie and the cockatiel, the two most popular pet parrots, come from central Australia. The ones in cages, though, are all bred in captivity.

RAINBOW LORIKEET *(TRICHOGLOSSUS HAEMATODUS)*, AUSTRALIA, NEW GUINEA AND EASTERN INDONESIA

MALLEE FOWL *(LEIPOA OCELLATA)*, SOUTHERN AUSTRALIA

▲ WHY DOES THE MALLEE FOWL BUILD A MOUND?
The mallee fowl buries its eggs in a huge mound of sand and rotting leaves.

The mallee fowl doesn't build a nest or sit on its eggs. Instead, the male builds a giant compost heap 5 m (16 feet) across. He takes care of it for ten hours every day, ten months a year. When the mound is ready, the female lays her eggs in it, and never bothers with them again.

For two months, the male keeps the temperature at almost exactly 33°C (96°F) by adding rotting plants or taking them away. It uses the inside of its beak as a thermometer to check its work. When the eggs hatch, though, his job is done. The babies dig their way out of the mound themselves and set off on their own. They can fly from the day they hatch.

HOW CAN I LEARN ABOUT AUSTRALIAN WILDLIFE?
If you live in Australia, you or your school can join the Gould League. There are branches in every state. The league has information on Australian wildlife and runs a competition for school students every year. Every October it runs a "Bird Day" when students and teachers count birds in their area. You can write to the Gould League of New South Wales at P.O. Box 150, Beecroft, NSW 2119.

▶ WHEN IS A BEAR NOT A BEAR?
When it's a koala! Koalas are related to kangaroos, not to bears.

Koalas look like little bears, but they are really marsupials – animals that carry their young in pouches. Kangaroos, possums and wombats are all marsupials. A baby koala stays in its mother's pouch for seven months. Then it rides on her back for four more months.

Koalas eat leaves, usually from eucalyptus trees. Eucalyptus leaves take a long time to digest, so the koala holds them in its appendix. A koala's appendix is a bag 2 m (6 feet) long running from its intestine. Compare that to your appendix, which is only the size of your little finger!

KOALA *(PHASCOLARCTOS CINEREUS)*, EASTERN AUSTRALIA

WHAT ABOUT...?
Where else can you find marsupials?
See page 75.

MAKING ROOM FOR WILDLIFE

Disappearing Wildlife

All over the world, wildlife is disappearing. People are responsible. We are cutting down forests, destroying coral reefs, and ruining other habitats wild animals and plants need. We spill oil into the sea, killing seabirds and other ocean creatures.

Because we want things animals have – their horns, their fur or their shells – we have killed so many that whole species have become extinct. Sometimes we even love wildlife to death. Because we want pet birds or fishes in our houses, or rare plants in our gardens, we pay people to take thousands of them away from the wild where they belong.

If we want to save wildlife, we will have to change our ways.

OLM *(PROTEUS ANGUINUS)*, CAVES IN SOUTHEASTERN EUROPE, RARE

▼ WHY ARE RHINOS DISAPPEARING?
Rhinoceros horn is worth a lot of money in parts of Asia. Thousands of rhinos have been killed to get it.

Rhinoceros "horn" is made of the same material as your fingernails. Nonetheless, many people in eastern Asia believe it is a good medicine for fever. In Yemen, men like to own rhino horn dagger handles. As a result, one rhino horn can be sold for thousands of dollars.

Many black rhinoceros have been shot by poachers, even though it is against the law to kill them or sell their horns. Today, all five species of rhinoceros are in danger of extinction. They will disappear soon unless people stop using rhino horn.

HOW CAN I HELP PROTECT WILDLIFE?
There are many ways. One good way is to make sure that if your family buys a pet, it is not an animal that was trapped in the wild. Wild animals are hard to keep alive. Because some of the animals that are caught die on their way to the pet store, trappers have to take extra animals from their natural homes so that some will live long enough to sell. This means that when you buy one, it means many more will be taken from their natural homes. It's better to choose an animal that has been bred as a pet for years, like a dog, a cat, a canary, a hamster or a budgie. You can adopt one from your local animal shelter.

BLACK RHINOCEROS *(DICEROS BICORNIS)*, AFRICA SOUTH OF THE SAHARA

▶ WHY DO OIL SPILLS KILL SEABIRDS?
Oil destroys the waterproofing on seabird feathers. It may also kill the fishes that they eat.

Most seabirds have a waterproof coating on their feathers that acts like a raincoat, keeping their skin warm and dry. If oil gets on their feathers, it destroys the coating. The birds may die from the wet and the cold. If they try to clean themselves, they end up swallowing oil that may poison them.

Spilled oil doesn't have to touch a seabird to harm it. A spill may kill off fishes and other animals seabirds need to eat. Oil sinking to the bottom may ruin an area for wildlife for many years.

OILED COMMON LOON OR GREAT NORTHERN DIVER *(GAVIA IMMER),* NORTHERN NORTH AMERICA, GREENLAND AND ICELAND

WHAT ABOUT...?
Why is the giant panda so rare?
See page 79.

◀ WHY IS THE THICK-BILLED PARROT IN DANGER?
These parrots are trapped to be sold as pets, and the forests where they live are being destroyed.

Thick-billed parrots live in the pine forests of northern Mexico. These forests are being cut down for their wood and to clear land for mining. The parrots need old trees with holes in them for nesting, but such trees are getting harder to find.

Like many parrots, thick-bills are also threatened by trappers who catch the birds to sell as pets. To-day, birds taken from trappers are being set free in Arizona, USA, where the thick-billed parrot once lived and where it may, at last, be safe.

THICK-BILLED PARROT *(RHYNCHOPSITTA PACHYRHYNCHA),* ARIZONA AND NORTHERN MEXICO

What Are People Good For?

Not everything we do to other creatures is bad. Some animals and plants are better off today because of us. People provide them with more food, shelter or growing space than they could ever find in the wild.

People can also help save endangered species. Sometimes all we have to do is stop hunting them or destroying their homes. Sometimes we have to work hard to help them have more babies or to build them new homes. When we do, we may find that some wonderful creatures will live right along with us.

▼ **HOW DO RACCOONS USE PEOPLE?**
Raccoons find food in the garbage people throw away, even in the middle of a big city.
The North American raccoon will eat almost anything, including fruit, fish, nuts, meat, eggs and corn. It is very intelligent, and it can use its front paws almost like hands. No wonder it has become an expert at raiding our garbage cans.

Though many of them still live in the woods, raccoons are one of the few mammals bigger than a rat or mouse to have done well in cities. In national parks, many raccoons have learned to beg for food from human visitors. Raccoons are actually more common today than they were a hundred years ago.

WHAT ABOUT...?
What are locusts?
See page 30.

RACCOON
(PROCYON LOTOR),
NORTH AMERICA

▶ HOW DID PEOPLE SAVE THE PEREGRINE FALCON?

The peregrine falcon was saved when North Americans stopped using a poison called DDT. Today, peregrine falcons even nest on our buildings.

Twenty years ago, the peregrine falcon, one of the fastest birds in the world, almost vanished from North America. They were being poisoned by DDT, a chemical farmers sprayed on their crops to kill insects. The poison made the peregrines lay eggs with such thin shells that they broke when their parents sat on them.

Many countries have now banned DDT, and the peregrines' numbers are growing again. Unfortunately, DDT is still used in other countries. Many other birds, like storks, are still being poisoned by DDT.

In the wild, peregrines nest on cliffs, but some scientists have encouraged them to use tall buildings instead. In a few cities, like Montreal, Canada, peregrines nest in the middle of the downtown area.

PEREGRINE FALCON *(FALCO PEREGRINUS)*, WORLDWIDE

▶ HOW ARE WE TRYING TO SAVE THE CRESTED TOAD?

Crested toads are being raised in zoos. Scientists are trying to put them back into the wild.

The crested toad lives on the island of Puerto Rico in the Caribbean Sea. For a long time, no one could find any. Then a few living toads were discovered by some young boys. They were taken to zoos in Canada and the United States, where they had hundreds of children and grandchildren. Now, some toads are being returned to a special place in Puerto Rico where they will be protected. We don't know yet if they will survive there.

It's better to save endangered species in the wild. But for some animals, like the crested toad, a good zoo can give them a last chance to survive.

HOW CAN I SHARE MY HOME WITH WILDLIFE?

You can help make your home into a wildlife refuge.

You can put up bird feeders or bat houses. You can plant flowers in your garden that attract butterflies, or food plants for their caterpillars. Remember not to spray them with poisons. Look at the reading list for books with ideas and instructions. Get your whole family to help!

CRESTED TOAD *(PELTOPHRYNE LEMUR)*, PUERTO RICO

What Can I Do to Help?

Saving the world's wildlife will be a long, hard job, but it's a job everyone can do. You don't have to be a famous scientist or a world leader to help. You don't even have to be a grownup. Children have helped save tropical rainforest, rescue injured animals, plant trees and clean up the environment.

You have already seen, in the earlier pages of this book, some ways you can help. You can probably think of others yourself, or find them in books or in newspapers or on television. Just remember that you can make a difference.

■ HOW WILL I KNOW WHAT TO DO?

The most important thing you can do to help our planet is to learn all you can about it. Then you can teach other people to save it.

The more you know about what is happening to wild animals and plants, the more you will be able to help them live. Books like this one are a good place to start. But if you want to find out what is going on right now, you should look for stories about wildlife in your newspaper, or on the radio or television news.

If you hear about something bad happening to wild animals or plants, or to the places where they live, tell your parents or your teacher. Write a letter to your member of parliament or congress, telling him or her how you feel. Perhaps your whole class can write letters and send them together. You can make a real difference!

■ CAN I START MY OWN NATURE CLUB?

Of course you can! One way to get started is to join "Roots and Shoots."

Dr. Jane Goodall is a famous scientist who has spent more than thirty years studying chimpanzees. She has started a new program for children called "Roots and Shoots." Members of Roots and Shoots can get help in starting their own club in their school or neighborhood, with ideas on how to study nature and help the environment. Write to The Jane Goodall Inter-Canada Association, 5165 Sherbrooke Street West, Montreal, Quebec, H4A 1T6.

Even if you don't want to join Roots and Shoots, you can always get together with your friends to help wildlife. Ask your teacher for ideas!

Glossary

Here are the meanings of some of the words in this book. Words in **bold face** *have their own entries in this glossary.*

Adaptation: The way animals and plants change to fit in with their environment.

Antarctic: The cold land from the South Pole north to the shores of the Southern Ocean, and the cold seas and islands around it.

Arctic: The lands and ocean at the "top of the world," from the North Pole south to the tree line, the farthest north that trees can grow. *See also* **Tundra**.

Carnivorous: Any animal or plant that eats meat is carnivorous. Plant-eating animals are called herbivorous.

Coral reef: A ridge or mound under the sea, made mostly out of the skeletons of coral animals.

Endangered species: An animal or plant that is in danger of becoming **extinct** soon.

Evolution: Change in animals and plants that is passed on from generation to generation.

Extinct: A **species** of animal or plant becomes extinct when the last one dies.

Habitat: The kind of place where an animal or plant lives. Forests, deserts, grasslands and coral reefs are habitats. So are smaller places, such as the top of a forest tree or inside a coral colony.

Insect: Insects are animals with **skeletons** on the outside, a body divided into three sections, and six legs. Beetles, dragonflies, grasshoppers, butterflies, bees and ants are insects. Spiders are not. Spiders have eight legs, not six, and their bodies are divided into two sections, not three.

Mammal: Mammals are animals that have fur or hair and feed their babies with milk. Kangaroos, lions, elephants, mice, seals, deer, rabbits, bats and whales are mammals (yes, whales have a few hairs on their bodies). So are we.

Marsupial: Marsupials are **mammals** that raise their young in pouches.

Mating: Animals mate when the sperm of the male joins with the egg of the female to produce a new individual. *See also* **Pollination**.

Pollination: Pollination happens when the male pollen joins with the female ovule to form the beginning of a new seed.

Predator: An animal, or plant, that kills and eats other animals. A predator is **carnivorous**, but a carnivorous animal is not necessarily a predator. A flea, for example, eats bits of a dog but does not hunt and kill it. It is a parasite, not a predator.

Prey: An animal that is eaten by a predator.

Primate: The primates are the group of **mammals** that includes lemurs, monkeys, apes, people and their relatives.

Rainforest: A rainforest is a forest where there is a lot of rain all year round. Its trees stay green all year. Not all rainforests are in the tropics, but the ones with the most kinds of animals and plants are.

Skeleton: The part of an animal's body that supports it. It may be on the inside of the body, like ours, or on the outside, like an insect's.

Species: A group of animals or plants that can mate with each other and have babies, but usually cannot mate with members of other species. Usually, when we talk about a "kind" of animal or plant, like a tiger or a sugar maple, we mean a species.

Territory: Any area that an animal, or a group of animals like a wolf pack, defends against other animals of its own kind. Some animals defend the whole area, or home range, in which they live. Others only defend a small area around their mate or their nest.

Tropics: The tropics are the warm parts of the world on either side of the equator.

Tundra: Land in the **Arctic** or a few places near the **Antarctic**, or high in mountains (alpine tundra), where the soil under the ground stays frozen all year.

Other Books to Read

There are many good books about wildlife for young readers. Here are just a few of them:

Series:

Eyewitness Books.
London: Dorling Kindersley.
There are many books in the Eyewitness series about animals and plants.

Great Creatures of the World.
Sydney: Weldon Owen.
This is a series of very good books adapted for children from another series for grownups. Titles include *Sharks; Alligators and Crocodiles; Dolphins and Porpoises; Sharks; Whales;* and *Elephants.*

Natural History Series.
Toronto: Key Porter Books.
Titles so far in this series include *Eagles; Wolves; Bears; Seals, Elephants,* and *Snakes.*

Individual Titles:
Burnie, David.
How Nature Works.
London: Dorling Kindersley, 1991.
One hundred experiments you can do to learn about nature.

Dewan, Ted, and Steve Parker.
Inside the Whale and Other Animals.
London: Dorling Kindersley, 1992.
Spectacular paintings show you how many animals are put together inside.

Doubilet, Anne.
Under the Sea from A to Z.
New York: Crown Publishers, 1991.
Not just an alphabet book! This book has beautiful underwater photography and lots of information about sea creatures.

Goodman, Billy.
A Kid's Guide to How to Save the Animals.
New York: Avon Books, 1991.
This book tells you about the ways people are trying to save animals, with ideas about how you can help.

Earthworks Group.
50 Simple Things Kids Can Do to Save the Earth.
Kansas City: Andrews and McMeel, 1990.
Here are things you can do every day to make this a better planet for all of us to live in, animals and plants included!

Goodall, Jane.
The Chimpanzee Family Book.
London: Picture Book Studio, 1989.
Jane Goodall introduces you to a family of wild chimpanzees that she has studied in Africa. This book is one of a series; look for *The Elephant Family Book* by Oria Douglas-Hamilton, 1990.

Hickman, Pamela.
Birdwise and **Plantwise.**
Toronto: Kids Can Press, 1988 and 1991.
Two books full of ideas on how to learn more about nature by yourself.

Lilly, Kenneth, illustrator.
The Animal Atlas.
London: Dorling Kindersley, 1992.
An atlas of world wildlife, with many illustrations of strange creatures from around the globe.

Opler, Paul.
Butterflies East & West.
Niwot, Colorado: Roberts Rinehart, 1993.
An activity and coloring book about North American butterflies and how to learn about them.

Payne, Katharine.
Elephants Calling.
New York: Crown Publishers, 1992.
The scientist who discovered that elephants use sounds too low for people to hear tells the story of one elephant family she studied in Africa.

Schneck, Marcus.
Your Backyard Wildlife Garden.
Toronto: Key Porter, 1993.
This is really a book for grownups, but you should tell your parents about it if you want your garden to be your private nature reserve.

Tyrrel, Esther Quesada.
Hummingbirds: Jewels in the Sky.
New York: Crown Publishers, 1992.
This book has some of the best photographs of hummingbirds ever taken.

Keep your eye out for **ZOOBOOKS.** Each ZOOBOOK magazine is about one kind or family of animals. They are very well written and illustrated. You can buy them separately, or subscribe.

Index

Numbers in italics refer to photographs.